RADICAL SMALL GROUPS

Reshaping Community to
Accelerate Authentic Life Change

by David Slamp

Copyright © 2014 David Slamp

All rights reserved.

Published by Made For Success Publishing
        P.O. Box 1775
        Issaquah, WA 98027

In accordance with the U.S. Copyright Act of 1976, the scanning, uploading, and electronic sharing of any part of this book without the permission of the publisher constitutes unlawful piracy and theft of the author's intellectual property. If you would like to use material from the book (other than for review purposes), prior written permission must be obtained by contacting the publisher at serive@MadeForSuccess.net. Thank you for your support of the author's rights.

All Scripture quotations, unless otherwise indicated, are from the Holy Bible, New International Version, Copyright © 1973, 1978, 1984 by International Bible Society. Used by permission.

Cover and Design by DeeDee Heathman

Library of Congress Cataloging-in-Publication Data
Slamp, David
    Radical Small Groups: Reshaping Community to Accelerate Authentic Life Change
    p. cm.-
    Includes biographical referrences and index.
    ISBN: 978-1-61339-659-9
    LCCN: 2014941490
    1. Christian Ministry / Discipleship - Religion. 2. Christian Ministry / Pastoral Resources - Religion. 3. Christian Church / Leadership - Religion. 4. Christian Ministry / Adult - Religion

For ordering information, please contact Made For Success Publishing
+14255266480

Foreword

Authentic life change does not "just happen". It can't be microwaved and it is not instant. We are transformed spiritually when we become believers, but living out that commitment is quite another challenge. It's been said, "Attending church does not make someone a Christian any more than sitting in a garage makes them a car." To be a vital believer we must live out our faith, actually applying what we say we believe. The most effective way to do that is to focus on life change within community.

While every ministry setting in the church world today has its strengths and value, no one setting does everything we need to make us authentic disciples. For example, in weekend services we are exposed and explained what the Bible **says and means**. In a small group we experience and express how to **apply and Live it out**. Even better, when we commit to both settings, we are informed, instructed, involved **and** impacted with the Word. This is putting into practice Acts 5:42, the normative form of Church; "Temple Courts" (weekend services) and "house to house" (small groups).

Many congregations today believe that one approach to making disciples or another is the best way. They chose to concentrate on that one and emphasize the method that appears to be the best. For one church it may be Bible studies and Sunday school. For another it is personal one-to-one discipleship. For yet another, small groups is the "way to go". In *Radical Small Groups* Dave Slamp shows us how to combine the best of these for maximum life transforming impact.

For 12 years David Slamp and I have known each other and shared our mutual passion for life transformation that happens best in small groups. In this book he has amplified the importance of authentic life change and shows us how to build healthy small groups into a more comprehensive approach to discipleship. The results are amazing! I know you will love the latest learnings, I did!

Steve Gladen
Pastor of Small Groups, Saddleback Church
Author of Small Groups with Purpose and
Leading Small groups with Purpose

Introduction

Welcome to *Radical Small Groups!*

A few years ago there was a big gap—a "chasm," if you will--between Sunday school and small group models and strategies. One could walk into any Christian book store and see two isolated sections of literature in each field. Conferences commonly focused on one or the other approach to create authentic disciples. Pastors and church leaders seemed convinced that one setting or the other was the "right" or "best" way to "make disciples."

Radical Small Groups bridges this gap and focus on the end objective: life change via the Sunday school, Bible study, and Small Group together. Each approach has unique strengths. When offered side by side, they accelerate the disciple making process! The result: radical life transformation! This combination celebrates the synergism between teaching and discipleship functions and produces vital spiritual growth.

Believers today face the weakness of a technological and highly impersonal society. Many people have "friends," but not true fellowship. They know *about* each another, but do not know each other. In other words, they are intimate strangers. Dealing with life struggles single-handedly people feel empty, alienated, and alone. This distance militates against true spiritual growth, as individuals struggle alone-- acting as though they are spiritually healthy, confident, and competent.

Radical Small Groups gives readers a clear and practical vision that will intensify authentic spiritual transformation. It helps serious and conscientious church leaders reshape community that will accelerate true life change!

Dave Slamp

What others are saying about Radical Small Groups...

"In Radical Small Groups Dave Slamp shows us how to combine the best of Sunday school, Bible studies, and small groups for maximum life-transforming impact!"

~Steve Gladen,
Pastor of small groups, Saddleback Church, Author of Small Groups with Purpose and Leading Small Groups with Purpose

"David Slamp lives what he writes! Our church was greatly enriched by his CareRing ministry. I heartily endorse it!"

~Dr. Stan Toler,
Pastor, General Superintendent Emeritus,
Church of the Nazarene and Author

"This is an excellent resources! You won't find any better tool!"

~C. Peter Wagner,
Author, Educator, Church Growth Expert, World Prayer Center

"Finally a book that does not take sides between the Sunday school class and small groups. Apply the 'passion' of CareRings to your church and begin working out these complimentary programs for outreach, teaching and the glory of God."

~Elmer L. Towns,
Author and educator, Dean of School of Religion, Liberty University

"What to do with Sunday School? David has helped us leverage Sunday school for small groups through his ideas and experience."

~Russ Robinson,
Director of Small Groups, Willow Creek Community Church

"David Slamp steps 'outside the box' challenging church leaders to rethink the insolated approach to small groups ... and the result will dramatically impact spiritual life in your church!"

~ Dr. Jim Garlow,
Lead Pastor, Skyline Church, San Diego

"This is a much needed resource in the Church throughout Africa. I highly recommend Radical Small Groups to all pastors committed to true biblical methods for strengthening discipleship ministry in their local churches.»

~Dr. Filimao Chambo,
Africa Regional Director, Church of the Nazarene

Dedication

*To my wife, Kathy, who lives her
Christian life as a true disciple
and shepherd of others.*

Table of Contents

Introduction **11**
  Adventure in CareRings 11
Chapter One **15**
  Indispensable Ministry 15
Chapter Two **37**
  The Amazing Power of Groups 37
Chapter Three **55**
  CareRings in Context 55
Chapter Four **71**
  A New Reformation 71
Chapter Five **83**
  Mission Accomplished 83
Chapter Six **93**
  A Perfect Match 93
Chapter Seven **111**
  Let's Get Organized! 111
Chapter Eight **125**
  First Steps 125
Chapter Nine **143**
  Decisions, Decisions 143
Chapter Ten **157**
  Your Other Job 157
Chapter Eleven **173**
  A Wagon Built on the Go 173
Chapter Twelve **193**
  The Never-Ending Adventure 193
Appendices **211**
Notes **224**
Bibliography **228**
About the Author **230**

Introduction:
Adventure in CareRings

Welcome to an adventure in CareRing! Here we hope to explore and understand what small groups are all about. We need to see the biblical significance of small groups and understand what they can and can *not* do. For some new to the adventure, these are "uncharted waters." Don't be afraid! Come on in; the water's fine. We want to introduce you to an ancient, yet vital ministry. Small groups are as old as Scripture itself, and as timely as the morning newspaper. They focus on relationships with others and are centered in the eternal Word of God. They work well–VERY WELL–with the Sunday school. Let's begin with a brief story about my friend, Don.

Don is in a small group made up primarily of men and women who attend the singles Sunday school class in his church. About three months into the meetings, Brett, a friend of Don's from work, confessed to Don that he had AIDS due to homosexual activity. Don was taken aback by this news but tried to be supportive and encouraging to Brett about turning his life over to Christ. He invited Brett to his small group, known as a CareRing. Brett agreed to come to the group, but first he wanted the group to know he had AIDS.

When Don passed the information on to his fellow group members, they talked about how they needed to show caring to others as Jesus did to the lepers of his day. Then they unanimously agreed to make Don's friend a part of the group. So Brett began coming regularly to the CareRing group–and eventually to the singles Sunday school class as well. Over a period of two months, Brett had many questions, which Don tried to answer. Brett came from an unchurched background and had no knowledge of Jesus and the plan of salvation, but he was deeply impressed by the love, prayers and caring attitudes of these people.

One night Don was driving Brett home and sharing Christ with him. He told Brett that with Christ in his heart he could start over right then and asked him if he would like to do that. Brett jumped at the opportunity. "Sure! Who wouldn't?" They pulled off to the side of the road and Don led Brett to Christ as the two of them prayed together with tears of repentance and joy.

For about six months, Brett attended the group and Don's church and then returned home to find a job. He remained there, continuing to live for God until his recent death.

***

There are hundreds in the world around us who, like Brett, have ruined their lives and desperately need God's love, forgiveness and power to cope with the consequences of their sins. Many of them don't know where to turn. They would respond to God if they could see his people living the Christian life up close but, sadly, many never get the chance.

We have to reach them! Few–far too few–are coming to us. So we have to take the Gospel to them. And that's where small groups come in.

> *Small groups give people a place and room to find the unconditional love they need.*

My friend Rick Ryding says, "Small groups give people a place and room to find the unconditional love they need." He's absolutely right. (By the way, the story of Don and Brett and their small group is true. Don is another personal friend.)

If you're still uncertain about whether small groups are a good idea, think for a minute about how Jesus operated. Jesus called out a few of his followers and prayed with them, led them and opened the Word to them. Then he sent them out to do the same. Small groups follow this same pattern. They offer one way to fulfill the mandate of Matthew 28:19-20: "Therefore, go and make disciples of all nations, baptizing them in the name of the Father and of the Son and of the Holy Spirit, and teaching them to obey everything I have commanded you."

This book is all about small groups that really work, and especially about the small groups called CareRings. (They are called CareRings because they are circles, or "rings," of caring people.) What sets CareRings apart from other kinds of small groups is that they are designed to be operated side by side with the existing adult education ministry of a local church. A Sunday

> *What sets CareRings apart from other kinds of small groups is that they are designed to be operated with the existing adult education ministry of a local church.*

school is a relatively formal learning environment, held in a church building, where time and opportunities for interaction are limited. A CareRing is a small group, usually meeting in a home, where people can build relationships with one another and help each other become better disciples of Jesus. By participating in Sunday school and CareRings, church members can become more like Christ in both head and heart.

It makes sense to develop groups alongside the Sunday school. As we will discuss in depth later, Sunday worship offers us the setting in which to listen to the Word. Sunday school is the best setting to learn from the Word, but groups are the best setting in which to learn to live by the Word. What we hear in church and understand in Sunday school can be applied in groups.

> *Sunday school is the best setting to learn from the Word, but groups are the best setting in which to learn to live by the Word.*

From a church's perspective, integrating small groups with Sunday schools is a great way to encourage growth in both areas. It's like what businesses call "synergy"–when one product line is used to build sales for another product line. Of course, a church is very different from a business. But, as we saw in the story of Don and Brett, a small group can be a way of getting a new person involved in Sunday school. And it can work the other way as well: a Sunday school class can become a point of entry to a small group. Churches that believe in the value of *both* traditional Christian education *and* small groups can build both ministries–and therefore have a greater impact on their members–by integrating the two. That's the CareRings way.

When I began this ministry ten years ago, there was nothing published on the subject of combining small groups with Sunday school. To my knowledge, that is still true today. And so I have written CareRings–Small Groups and Sunday School Side by Side to help churches of all sizes start small groups where there are already strong adult Sunday school classes. More than 200 churches of all evangelical denominations nationwide are using CareRings, and the movement is spreading.

For some this book is a beginning, a first taste of small group ministry. If that's true for you, I hope it will be the beginning of further reading and searching that will blossom into a powerful, life-changing ministry. For others this book is the extension of an earlier interest in small groups. I pray you will grow your interest and deepen your commitment to be about the Father's business. May God bless and empower you for the vital work of loving others, applying God's Word to your life and praying from your heart with one another in a small group.

So now it's time to get started. The rest of this book will take you step-by-step through all of the basics of starting a productive CareRing small group ministry in your church. When you're finished reading it, you'll want to get the companion pieces as well–CareRings Training Workbook and CareRings Bible Studies (a collection of 52 weeks of small group lessons), both available from the author.

WELCOME TO THIS GREAT ADVENTURE IN CARERING!

Chapter One:
Indispensable Ministry: Why Every Church Should Have Small Groups

Small group ministry is not a "program." That is, it is not just some promising new activity you add on to your church's already long list of activities and maybe drop later when something better comes along. It truly is a *ministry*, a fundamental part of what it means to be a spiritual body living in the presence of God. Churches that understand what small groups are all about would no more look at this ministry as a mere activity option than they would look at corporate worship as optional.

> *... a fundamental part of what it means to be a spiritual body living in the presence of God.*

Small group ministry is a spiritual experience that we all need, and we must resolve to keep it that way through prayer, faithfulness to God and honest confession. If we let it degenerate into a mere program, it is doomed.

Because small groups are not a program but a ministry, you should not look at this book as providing an exact blueprint that you can build from directly in your own church. Indeed, it is never enough to import some plan that worked elsewhere and simply plug it into your own situation, believing God will bless it. He may, of course. But the reason a plan worked elsewhere was because God was in control. I have known many churches that have tried some approach because they were excited about someone else's story, only to experience disaster in their own congregation when trying to replicate that approach. So be smart and use this book as a source of information that you will adapt for your own situation. Always submit your ideas, planning and working with the leading of the Holy Spirit. If God is in your small group ministry, leading you in the process, you will be effective!

FIVE "FIRM PRINCIPLES"

Having given out that caution, I nevertheless want to begin with five basic principles that I believe to be universal for all successful small group ministries.

1. The small group ministry must have foundational support from the top leader. The pastor may assume the leadership of the small group ministry or he/she may find a mature leader among the congregation who will do it. Whichever is the case, the pastor must make a public statement along these lines: "This new small group ministry is something I am confident God is pleased with and I have made a long-term commitment to it." He/she must back up his words with action.

2. Small group ministry leaders must be flexible–but not too flexible–when enlisting members. When we're starting small groups and encouraging people to join them, we have to be patient. Some people will respond almost immediately to the idea (typically about 10 percent); others will think a while before getting involved (about 80 percent); and still others will never get involved (about 10 percent). So we need to give that middle 80 percent of our people time to make up their minds while we keep applying gentle pressure to join a small group.

> *If they are trained, almost all people can become sensitive, capable small group leaders.*

3. Groups must have trained leaders. If they are trained, almost anyone can become sensitive, capable small group leaders. Many assume they are already equipped to lead a small group because they teach Sunday school, teach in a public school or do some form of counseling related to their work. It is true that many skills used in those settings will put one ahead in leading small groups. But individual participation, shepherding skills and discovery learning are so essential to small groups that it is necessary to have training specifically in leading such groups. Training should be offered at a variety of times.

Some can attend on Saturday, others need an evening training setting during the week, but still everyone needs quality training.

4. Groups must keep a balance among Bible application, prayer and fellowship. If a group emphasizes study of the Word too much, they will overlook those new to the group whom they are trying to reach. Similarly, if a group emphasizes prayer too much, the group will lose sight of everything but their own concerns. And if a group loves its fellowship too much, they will accomplish little. All three–Bible study, prayer and fellowship–are valuable and should be kept in balance.

5. Groups must focus on outreach and evangelism. The natural tendency in a group is to become close to each other and overlook the greater purpose–to reach out and win the lost to Jesus. We must consistently keep this purpose in focus. We are not saved to sit. We are not sanctified to study. We are redeemed to reach out.

> *We are not saved to sit. We are not sanctified to study. We are redeemed to reach out.*

With these basic principles in mind, we can move on to consider why every church should have a small group ministry. We'll learn that the Bible supports the small group approach, that small groups meet basic human needs, and that small groups form one of the three primary settings of church life.

THE BIBLICAL BASIS FOR SMALL GROUPS

The basis of any ministry in the Christian community is the Bible. The Bible is the Word of God, the revelation of his will and plan. Scripture is loaded with teachings, illustrations and examples of those principles that form the basis of small groups. The following examples are only some of the many that are available. Let's begin in the Old Testament.

Moses and the Power of Delegation

Exodus 18 tells a story to which small group ministry leaders should pay attention. The place was the Sinai Peninsula. The time was during the forty years of wandering in the wilderness after Moses led the children of Israel out of Egypt. Moses was acting as a judge, or arbiter of disputes, for all of the vast company of the Hebrews.

Moses' father-in-law, Jethro, visited him and observed that the demands on Moses were far too great. The Hebrew leader was laboring from morning till night at making all sorts of judgments. So Jethro suggested that Moses appoint judges–men who were trustworthy and who feared God–to lead groups and families in making decisions. In other words, he recommended that Moses institute a sort of judicial bureaucracy to spread out the workload. Moses saw the wisdom in this and did as his father-in-law had suggested.

Commentators are not in full agreement about how this actually worked. But apparently the Hebrew people were broken down into small segments, with a hierarchy of judges put in place so that no single judge–including Moses himself–had more than a small number of persons he was responsible for. We might call this the "10/10 concept," in which a judge over a thousand persons, for example, was directly responsible for only ten judges lower in the hierarchy.

Exactly how it worked out is incidental. The structure was clearly one of organized labor and shared leadership. And the plan worked. It had the advantages of sparing the leader, sharing the decision-making process and putting scores of men–perhaps hundreds of them–in places of leadership.

Note that Moses was still the supreme leader. Jethro told him to continue teaching the people the decrees and laws of God and to show them how to live. He was to do the selection of the judges and he continued to bring difficult cases before God. There was nothing threatening to Moses' leadership about this new organization he put in place. In fact, it was good for him. I have often wondered if this plan was one of the reasons he could continue to actively serve until the age of 120!

The church today needs pastors who can catch the "10/10" vision of shared spiritual leadership. Pastors need to continue teaching and preaching the truth, and the community must always be responsible to and respectful of pastors. But if we are to increase our effectiveness, we must enlist more leaders and empower them to help carry the load under the overall leadership of their pastors.

This can be done effectively through small groups. Indeed, the most effective means of equipping lay leaders and empowering them to serve is by having them shepherd from eight to ten people whom they love, teach, care for and pray with.

Small groups expert Carl George recently responded to one person's question, "If I had to choose, is it more important to develop small groups in my church or train leaders?" George responded that the more important task is to train strong lay leaders. He added that the best way to develop leaders is with small groups.

> *The best way to develop leaders is with small groups.*

When the sort of training George mentioned is carried out, it is remarkable to see laymen and women who have wanted for years to do something significant with their lives finally getting involved in ministry.

In the church where I served–Central Community Church in Wichita, Kansas–we have more than 150 such people trained to give care. They serve alongside the pastor and staff. Our pastor has personally endorsed them, and we presented them for dedication in a public worship service. They have been given a plaque to celebrate their training and to remind them of their responsibilities as lay ministers we call "shepherds." They each wear a gold shepherd's name tag on their lapel or dress every Sunday to say to the congregation, "Here is a person who is in a place of leadership, who has accepted training in caregiving, and who is available for counseling, prayer and discipleship."

It is a marvelous blessing to see them giving care and expressing their love to others in the fellowship. On occasion we see them with a friend, their heads bowed, praying together about a need or burden. They faithfully call new people to our church and follow up with any in their small group who are absent. The shepherds are the first ones to join a member of their group at the altar for prayer. They make hospital visits, share their resources, express love and perform a thousand other ministries. All of this would have to be done by the pastor or other staff members, if it were not for these precious men and women who serve faithfully.

Shared leadership, developed through small groups, is the only way to keep on meeting needs as a church grows.

Small but Mighty

Throughout Scripture we see how God used the "leftovers," the "has-beens" and the "have-nots" to confound the wise and defeat the powerful. He used a nomad named Abraham, a shepherd boy named David and an orchard worker named Amos. With ordinary people, God brings gain out of loss, freedom out of despair and victory out of defeat. Often it seems he intentionally chooses those with the least to lose. And perhaps therein lies the secret. The poor have no other source of help, the sick no other source of healing and the needy no other source of hope. So when God speaks, they respond in faith and simple obedience–and with them, God changes the world!

The same is true for those who are few in number. Time and again, the Bible shows us how God used little groups of people to perform mighty deeds.

It was that way with Gideon and his band of 300 men in the battle recorded in Judges 7. Early in the morning God told Gideon, "You have too many men for me to deliver Midian into their hands" (v. 2). It appears that Gideon could have done it by himself. With 33,000 troops, who needs God anyway? So 22,000 of them went home. Still too many. Eventually less than one-tenth of the original force was left to fight, but with that "remnant" God won the battle–and they knew it!

It was that way, as well, when David met Goliath (1 Sam. 17). The thousands of men in Saul's Israelite army were not enough to challenge the Philistine champion Goliath, because they were faithless. The right number for victory was one–David, a mere boy. Because of that one boy, armed with nothing more than a slingshot, the fearsome giant came tumbling down. One plus God is always a majority.

For Elijah on Mount Carmel, sixty words in a simple prayer of faith were all he needed. As we learn in 1 Kings 18, the prophets of Baal had cried, slashed and beaten themselves, wailing to deaf ears until they fell to the ground in the frenzy. But Elijah, standing alone, asked God to show his power. Elijah prayed a very simple prayer (other than the names he used, there were only four multisyllabic words in his prayer). But that one man and his simple request were working the will of God, and the fire fell.

We get it backwards. We believe bigger is automatically better. And when we're part of a big group we believe we can get the job done by ourselves. We don't need God! But small groups don't get overconfident (at least until they grow big and stay that way for too long). They know their effectiveness depends on God.

> *When God is involved, smaller is better and less is best.*

When God is involved, smaller is better and less is best.

House Churches of New Testament Times

The earliest Christians saw their homes as fit places in which to worship God and enjoy fellowship with one another. There was a time for public activity and there was a time to come together as fellow believers in the privacy of their homes. For example, Acts 2:46 tells us that the early Christians in Jerusalem "continued to meet together in the temple courts" and that "They broke bread in their homes and ate together with glad and sincere hearts." Similarly, in Acts 5:42 we read, "Day after day, in the temple courts and from house to house, they [the apostles] never stopped teaching and proclaiming the good news that Jesus is the Christ" (emphasis added). Thus, along with ministry among the crowds, quieter times spent within individuals' homes helped the early believers become people who were spiritually alive and in love with God and each other.

There is ample evidence from the New Testament that the early Christians around the Mediterranean met in what are today called "house churches." For example, in testifying about his time spent ministering in Ephesus, Paul said, "You know that I have … taught you publicly and from house to house" (Acts 20:20). And when writing to the

Roman believers, Paul sent his greeting to the church that met in the house of Priscilla and Aquila (Rom. 16:3-5).

It makes sense. When the early Christians were not allowed to preach Christ in the synagogues, they went into homes. A house provided a sheltered, comfortable place to meet. Only much later in history, when Christianity gained official status, did church buildings become part of the Christian experience.

Given that historical situation, it's important to note that the early Christian house churches must have been quite small—more like what we think of as small groups than what we think of as church congregations. Anyone who has been to Israel and visited excavation sites knows that the houses of the New Testament era were very small. In most cases, therefore, the churches must have been groups of only 12 to 20 believers.

Another observation backs up this idea of the house church. In the New Testament there is no word for "layperson." The New Testament does refer to special offices. It speaks of people being chosen for particular ministries and functions, but it communicates no idea of a distinction between the "clergy" and "laypeople."

Jesus called, taught and trained his disciples, not so they would just be with him, but because he intended to send them out two-by- two. Only later, as the church grew and developed over the years, did it become common practice for some to serve full time in ministry and to be "separated" (in one sense of the word) to that ministry.

> *No place in the New Testament do we see anyone sitting back to be served and ministered to.*

However, no place in the New Testament do we see anyone sitting back to be served and ministered to. Everyone performed service, work and ministry. So we find a food server named Stephen speaking to the Sanhedrin and being martyred as a result (Acts 6-7). An otherwise unknown disciple named Ananias placed his hands on the future missionary Saul, and Saul was converted (Acts 9:10-19). We read that "those who had been scattered by the persecution in connection with Stephen traveled as far as Phoenicia, Cyprus and Antioch, telling the message only to Jews" (Acts 11:19). First Peter 2:9 tells us, "But you are a chosen people, a royal priesthood, a holy nation, a people belonging to God, that you may declare the praises of him who called you out of darkness into his wonderful light."

If house-sized groups of ordinary people could set off the amazing growth spurt of the early church, then who knows what small groups of Christians meeting across the land can accomplish today?

Everyone Is a Minister

We will discuss later how church history affirms the place of spiritual giftedness and how Reformation theology implies a vital role of service and ministry for all saints (see chapter four). But for now we need to understand how the Christian community is intended to function. The analogy of the body does this best, since it is based on broad sections of Scripture and connects with the idea of ministry.

In perhaps the most remarkable use of the body analogy, 1 Corinthians 12 reveals that our existence is one of unity. Here Paul says, "For we were all baptized by one Spirit into one body ... and we were all given the one Spirit to drink" (v. 13). Likewise, in verse 25 Paul reminds us of God's plan that "so there should be no division in the body." Yet there is variety. "Now the body is not made up of one part but of many" (v. 14).

No one is excluded. "If the foot should say, 'Because I am not a hand, I do not belong to the body,' it would not for that reason cease to be part of the body" (v. 15). In fact, the body would not be able to function if every part did the same thing (that is, if all people performed the same ministry). God has put us all together just as he wants us to be. The parts that are the least obvious or "up front" in the expression of their service are indispensable.

Actually, God combined the members of the body in such a way as to give greater "honor" to the parts that lack it. Romans 12:6 explains, "We have different gifts, according to the grace given us." This means, among other things, that we should serve with gladness and sincerity however we have been gifted (Rom. 12:7–8).

Ephesians 4:11–16 shows the power of serving God and others the way he has empowered us. The function of the pastor-teacher is "to prepare God's people for works of service" (Eph. 4:12). The result of this is that "the body of Christ may be built up until we all reach unity in the faith and in the knowledge of the Son of God and become mature, attaining to the whole measure of the fullness of Christ" (Eph. 4:12–13).

Throughout this brief study, we come to see the "members of the body" as vital to the strength and maturity of the whole body. Each has a part, and every part and function is important to the whole. It goes without saying–although Scripture does say it–that Jesus is the head of the body, his church. We take our orders from him much like the muscles move at the impulse of the brain.

> *Every body grows by cell multiplication.*

There are other similarities between the church and the body. For example, every body grows by cell multiplication. You began as one cell that divided, with those two cells dividing again, and so on. Even now your body is imperceptibly and persistently forming new cells.

Much like the body, the church has "cells" that grow and multiply. We call healthy cells Bible studies, fellowships or groups. We sometimes refer to what appear to be unhealthy cells as "clubs" or "cliques." We do so with tongue in cheek, suggesting that they have separated themselves from the body.

While this can happen, it should not and does not need to happen. Literally, hundreds of thousands of people are in healthy small groups. One national survey suggests that there are an estimated 55,000 groups in America's churches. If each one averages about 12 members, that means no fewer than 750,000 Christians are in small groups today.

In one church, Skyline Wesleyan in San Diego, the Sunday school grew in one eight-year period from 400 to 1200–remarkable by anyone's standards. During that time, small groups also grew from none when they started to over 1400 in two years. If this can happen in fast-paced southern California, where you might think people would not have time for small groups, then it can happen anywhere.

KEY NEEDS THAT SMALL GROUPS CAN MEET

One reason we have small groups is that they reflect biblical teaching. Another reason is that they meet basic needs. Small groups serve important purposes in the life of a church and in the lives of the individuals within those small groups. Key needs met by small groups include: (1) the need to be a responsible Christian; (2) the need to help others in society; (3) the need to feel a sense of belonging; (4) the need to develop leaders for the church's work. Small groups have much practical value to offer us.

> *Hundreds of Christians ... know him and love him, but lack the structure in their lives to apply what they feel and know.*

The Need to Be Responsible Christians

Hundreds of Christians have a deep and gnawing hunger to follow through on their commitment to Christ. They know him and love him, but lack the structure in their lives to apply what they feel and know. Small groups provide this structure.

- ***Small groups help us reach non-Christians.*** Responsible Christians have a primary felt need to effectively contact non-Christians for the Lord. In our hearts we know we should be reaching lost men, women and children. We wholeheartedly agree that the church must be about the Father's business of seeking and saving those who are lost. We want to get on with it but lack either the know-how or the ongoing enthusiasm to sustain this part of the ministry.

- ***Small groups help us grow spiritually.*** Many Christians also have a desire for spiritual maturity. Yet while we agree that we need to advance spiritually, often we let the pursuit of spiritual maturity get crowded out of our lives by other concerns. Many believers have been conditioned to a passive faith so long that they have given up on growing. The old spiritual said it best. "We've been down so long, gitt'n up never crossed our minds!"

- **Small groups help us know one another better and care for each other.** When I was attending college, a fellow student named Bob Miller was a great cutup. I passed him on the way to a class one day and said the customary "Hi, Bob!" He answered, "Fine, thanks." I just laughed at the time, but thinking about it since then I have realized that Bob was making a statement. He cut through three paragraphs of perfunctory greetings to get to the final response. He reminded me that far too much of our communication takes place on the surface.

Some years ago the college where I taught installed computers in every office and dorm room on campus. As a part of the phase-in of the project, professors were invited to attend a few hours of training. One of the classes I attended was about using something new called the "Internet." While we were taking the class, the instructor offered us some options–projects we could do right there to connect to a variety of places. Within a few moments, I had on my screen the NASA handbook with complete information on how to become an astronaut. Minutes later, I could read the entire Shakespearean collection from the Dartmouth University Library on my screen. Amazing! At least it was then. We perform such tasks routinely today.

The truly amazing thing is that I could do all that–and much more–without ever seeing or talking with a person. No greeting, no smile, no handshake. Only a keyboard and computer screen. Many live through a typical day doing just that. This leaves them empty inside, missing the fellowship and personal touches that mean so much to us.

The point of all this is simply that we are not reaching people who are lost and bringing them into a relationship with Christ and the church. We are not growing spiritually and have accepted nongrowth as normative. We do not know one another as close friends. The result? We feel guilty (and some of us truly are guilty) for not reaching out more. Some are carrying more than their load–way more–and desperately need rest and revitalization. They are weary and even feel "used" by their own fellowships.

We need to build opportunities to get into contact with neighbors who do not know Christ. We need to structure settings in which we concentrate on spiritual maturity and faith development. We must create time in which to get to know one another–really know one other.

CareRings do exactly the things we have been talking about. Since they are in homes, we are moving the church out of the four walls of the sanctuary or Sunday school classroom and into our communities. We are not expecting the world to come to us. We are going into the world! That even sounds more Christian, doesn't it? We are reaching out to others, inviting them into our homes for fellowship and a Bible study.

> *CareRings build on the preaching ministry of the worship services and the teaching ministry of the Sunday school to apply the Word to our lives.*

CareRings build on the preaching ministry of the worship service and the teaching ministry of the Sunday school to apply the Word to our lives. When the Word is preached, it is exposed to us. When it is taught, it is explained to us. But when we gather around the Word in a small group, sharing our insights, *we are examined by it.*

CareRings provide a weekly setting in which to get to know each other. Instead of leaving fellowship to chance, we take the initiative and spend quality time with a few friends. The trust level begins to build as we maintain confidences, and in time, we find ourselves opening up, becoming vulnerable, sharing–and caring!

The Need to Help Society

We are not the only ones in need. We are part of a larger community. This includes the church but extends far beyond the church's concerns. We are part of an American society filled with deep human needs.

Much of the church in America developed in rural settings where there was community, trust and bonding with each other that developed over time through shared work, a common ethic and sense of family. Over the years, as people moved into the towns and cities, they lost the fine art of entertaining in their homes. The dining room gave way to the restaurant and the parlor to the conference room.

Similarly, we live in a transient society. Almost none of us lives in the same town or city where our grandparents were raised. We conclude, *If things are not right here, I'll leave. If they don't treat me right at my job, I'll find other work. If something I don't like happens at church, I'll move on.* We lack staying power. This is intensified by a consumer culture in which we all can demand service to our liking and go elsewhere if it is not granted–cheerfully. Greed causes us to go to extremes to be pleased, pampered and petted.

In the middle of this social struggle is one constant. Jesus is the one steady person in the universe. He and his people have been around–and will continue to be around–for centuries. As his representatives, we have an obligation to the society in which we live. Just as the family is the basic unit of society, so the small group is the basic unit of the church. Within a small group, closeness, trust and bonding can be reborn.

I recently read of a national study revealing that every year 53,000 people leave the church and never come back. Of that number, more than 85 percent left saying they did not feel accepted.[1] If even half of this is true, small groups are desperately needed to provide a sense of acceptance and approval.

> *Just as the family is the basic unit of society, so the small group is the basic unit of the church.*

The Need to Belong

Many of the unchurched sense within themselves an acute desire to be a part of something that is bigger than themselves and has eternal meaning. This is perhaps especially true of the baby busters. Among these adults born after 1960, many are growing weary of self-oriented materialism. But when they go in search of a church home, they don't necessarily find one that offers what they're looking for. They are notoriously slower to establish trust than their older counterparts. So, to make it comfortable for them, we need to move the church out into neighborhoods through small group ministry.

Groups offer people of all ages a place and regular opportunity to be a part of something. Through groups, we make the Christian community accessible to the world. We give the unchurched a convenient chance to be a part of something in a way that is natural to them.

This claim is supported by a historical observation offered by pastor and author Leith Anderson. First, he said, the Sunday school was the primary entry point for people to become a part of a Christian community in America. Next, the Sunday evening service became the door through which people entered a church body. But for most people today, says Anderson, weekday groups are the channel by which people join a church.[2]

Anderson's observation is an important one, and there is much evidence to back it up. For example, the abundance of literature about and for small groups has been steadily increasing. A decade ago, one would be fortunate to find

> *For most people today ... weekday groups are the channel by which people join a church.*

two or three resources about small groups in Christian bookstores. Today, it is not uncommon to find bookstores devoting whole sections to booklets covering different study topics, books containing ideas for small group development and even texts on small group theory.

Today it is easy to get personalized help with your church's small group ministry. Training seminars and nationwide conferences have proliferated. Many denominations have put leaders in place to facilitate their denominational small group ministries. I am personally asked to consult with churches of all sizes about small group ministry in general and CareRings in particular, once or twice a month! Parachurch organizations like Serendipity House focus on small groups.

One of the most probable reasons for this proliferation of group materials and personal guidance is that small group ministry is meeting a real need people feel for belonging.

The Need for Leadership Training

Every church that wants to keep growing *broader* through adding new members and to keep growing *deeper* in spirituality has an ongoing need to develop new leaders for new and old ministries. Where are these new leaders going to be identified and trained? As experience has shown, a small group is an excellent setting within which to train lay ministers for service and leadership.

In his provocative book *Unleashing the Church,* Frank R. Tillapaugh prodded the church out of the pew and into the marketplace. He echoed what Ray Stedman had said more than a decade earlier when he developed *Body Life* and the principles of lay ministry and leadership.[3] Richard Halverson made similar statements in *The Timelessness of Jesus Christ.* "The work of the church is outside the establishment. Outside the church. In the world. And it takes every member to do it! Nowhere in the Bible is the world exhorted to 'come to church.' But the church's mandate is clear: She must go to the world."[4] CareRings help Christians do just that!

> *The work of the church is outside the establishment. Outside the church. In the world. And it takes every member to do it!*

In a small group, you learn what the Word says and how to apply it. In a small group, others help you become more spiritually disciplined. In a small group, you have a chance to exercise your spiritual gifts. These are just the sorts of experiences that bring a person to a point of spiritual maturity where he or she can begin serving others through a position of leadership. Along with meeting the three needs to help people become responsible Christians, helping the larger society and feeling a sense of belonging, small groups can also meet at least some of the pressing need for leadership training.

THE THREE L'S OF CHURCH LIFE

We've already seen how small groups are consistent with biblical principles and have proved to be of great practical value. Now it is time to consider how a small group ministry fits into the overall structure of a church.

I've found it useful to think of a church as having three primary settings, each differing from the other two according to its purpose and design. These settings are the worship service, the educational ministry and the small group ministry. In a worship service we praise God and listen to the preaching of his Word. In Sunday school we receive and discuss biblical teaching that is vital to becoming persons knowledgeable in Christian truth. In small groups we experience intimacy with fellow believers, learn to apply scriptural teaching and develop a more powerful prayer life.

These three settings form what I call "the three L's" of evangelism and Christian nurture. These three settings involve, respectively: (1) listening to the Word; (2) learning from the Word; and (3) living by the Word.[5] All three functions–listening, learning and living–are vital to becoming more like Christ, and so all three settings are necessary in the life of a church.

Let's consider each setting in more depth.

Listening to the Word

In a worship service we read Scripture and hear a message presented from the Word. We begin understanding the message of the Bible. Here, too, we often take notes and follow the biblical admonition to "bring all the tithes into the storehouse" (Mal. 3:10, KJV) and to "make a joyful noise unto the LORD" (Ps. 98:4, KJV). We hear of God's power in the lives of those around us in the form of testimonies–both sung and spoken.

The primary function of this setting is praise and worship. We lift God's name and character up before others. We glorify him by singing songs, hymns and spiritual songs. Most importantly, we hear Scripture read and preached.

But therein lies the very need not addressed in this setting–accountability and intimacy. We hear the Gospel in a worship service, but this is not where we live it out. It is preached mostly here, but not practiced mostly here. And, really, it shouldn't be. We are told to "go out to the roads and country lanes and make them come in ..." (Luke 14:23). Jesus himself commanded us to "go into all the world and preach the good news to all creation" (Mark 16:15). Ultimately, the objective is to get others into the "flock" and into church. But first we must reach them. We must go.

> *We hear the Gospel in a worship service, but this is not where we live it out.*

One great advantage of the "listening" setting is that the size of the body doing the celebrating is unlimited. It started in the Old Testament with the first Passover during the Exodus and was continued with the Feast of Trumpets, the Feast of Tabernacles, and so on. It was always a national celebration. Great major events in the faith history of Israel were marked and remembered with these feasts.

There is a new feast now–the crowning event of the new covenant is the Resurrection! Jesus Christ won a final victory over sin, death, hell and the grave as he rose up to new life. This event provides the content in three of the first four messages ever preached by the church. And now Christians celebrate that victorious event on the day Christ arose–Sunday. It is a weekly celebration, not an annual one, for in Jesus' resurrection we enjoy perpetual liberty and freedom, both from sins and the punishment for them.

Each and every week that message is remembered and preached. The Word is central because it is the record of Jesus, the church and God's will for all who are Christians. This is the exposition of the Bible–that Jesus lives today and lives within us by grace through faith.

Nowhere is the Resurrection event and its power remembered more than on this sacred day.

Learning from the Word

Next, the "learning" setting is one in which we come to better understand the Scripture and its story. Here, it is explained to us as we read it, hear it and discuss it. Typically, we are exposed to a broader passage and hear a lesson explaining the meaning. More often than not, the room is set up with chairs in rows facing a podium, where the teacher stands to teach. The class uses a planned curriculum that walks us week-by-week through a personality study, a Bible book or a real-life topic. The Bible is referred to often. Normally, we gather for light talk, perhaps some coffee and doughnuts; we pray for needs mentioned; a lesson is taught and we discuss. The discussion generally falls into one of two categories:

- In the first category, class members talk about a common subject regarding personality, the social situation or some other life-related topic.

- The second category of discussion typically follows a lesson (or is part of it) in which students discuss the Scripture at hand with each person sharing their views. Some will describe events from their lives that illustrate the Scripture lesson. Others will share some view they read or heard discussed by someone else.

My wife and I visited a church in Texas and attended a Sunday school class much like this. The things they talked about in general were just that–general talking about things! No one except the teacher was particularly prepared for the lesson. The words spoken were not biblical insights shared by observant and sensitive people. They were more like a random conversation on everything from old wives' tales to hearsay to bits of pop theology. As my wife and I left the worship service, we agreed it was great. But the class had been little more than the pooling of ignorance.

This is not to say we didn't appreciate the views expressed in the class, nor to say that nothing of value was spoken in the class. Rather, it is a call to purposeful and constructive discussion. It is an urgent prodding that Sunday school teachers guide the conversation in their classes so that it be limited to specific topics and to Scripture. Also, it is an observation that too many classes have degenerated into little more than friendship circles or heated personal discussion sessions on controversial topics. This can–and needs to–be changed. Study of the Bible must once again become primary and central in Sunday school classes.

> *Too many classes have degenerated into little more than friendship circles or heated personal discussion sessions.*

Along with this, Sunday schools are limited by time, location and structure. Frequently, the lesson is given no more than 25 to 30 minutes. Its placement next to worship normally makes it more formal and structured. None of this is bad or should be changed necessarily. It's just the way it is.

Two other factors about the Sunday school are worth noting.

- First, the primary function of a Sunday school class is Bible study. Often there is no open sharing of insights on the scriptural topic, no extended prayer in which everyone participates, and no time for quality fellowship in which deep trust builds over a period of time.

- Second, the maximum size of a Sunday school class is about 30 (perhaps more where a class meets in a larger room). We tracked the history of a few classes in one church I pastored, only to find that at about 30 or 35 they plateaued–just stopped growing! The limiting factor was not the room space, a lack of teachers or problems with the location. In every case the limiting factor was the loss of significant, close, personal contact as the class grew. So in every case we started CareRings within each of those classes. The classes once again continued to grow–and so did the Sunday school!

In one denomination the average church has about 75 in worship attendance. It is probable that the limitations we are talking about here in the Sunday school also apply in the small church. People sometimes say something like "Our church is like a warm family. We all love one another and are so close to each other. I just hope we *never* grow!"

This is resistance to growth for fear of losing a sense of closeness and familiarity.

People need and often crave love, so it is only natural for them to want to preserve settings where they feel loved. Actually, this may be a factor that militates against reaching the lost. We get so attached to one another that we are afraid of being separated. So we close the group. In some extreme situations, people are selfish with each other. They reason that if there were "others" (newcomers) in the church, they would not be close with their friends.

One national study indicates that none of us knows more than about 60 people well in a local church. So it doesn't matter if the fellowship is 60 or 6,000. In the larger church we just need to structure times and set up places for sharing and discovering together.

Living by the Word

The final setting is the smallest. It is also the most personal. Because of this, it fits the tone of the times best–personal expression and individuality. In the group of from 10 to 12, everyone has a chance to pray, offer a biblical insight and share his or her life's joys, needs and sorrows. Everyone is seated in a circle and there is no obvious "leader." This again fills a hunger for teamwork, to be a part and to be appreciated.

Here, in the small group setting, we examine the Scripture and our lives to see where we can grow and mature. There is a sense of accountability to God and one another. We pray for each other, though none are ever "forced" to pray or read the Bible. Most importantly there is ownership. Everybody feels they are a part–and they are! Yet someone is trained to facilitate the discussion and keep it on track around some form of biblically-based application of the Word. This person is called the "Shepherd-Leader."

In the small groups called CareRings the main functions are prayer, personal intimacy and application of the Scripture to life. They are perfect for examination of our lives and reflection on what the Word has to say to us. The maximum size is 12 people, and CareRings meet in homes. There is closeness and intimacy that can't be fostered like this in any other setting.

There is always someone called an "apprentice" in every CareRing, who is there being mentored by the "shepherd-leader." These apprentices go through training early in their experience and get on-the-job training with constant encouragement and support. At first they take a minor role, perhaps reading some Scripture, praying a closing prayer or opening with an ice-breaker. Then, in a few weeks, they take a more central role, leading a portion of discussion or prayer dialogue.

About this time, you may be asking, "So what?" And that's a fair question. Exactly what is this all about? In short, this is all about relationships. Groups are about our relationships with each other. That's community. And groups are about our relationship with God. That's covenant. These two dimensions are brought together in CareRings because everything we do is for one of these two purposes: to enhance our fellowship with each other or to build our relationship with God.

> *Groups are about our relationships with each other. That's community. And groups are about our relationship with God. That's covenant.*

Summary of the Three L's

So there you have them: the listening, learning and living settings–the worship service; the education ministry; the small group ministry. Each works hand-in-hand with the others. To be complete–that is, to minister to the variety of human needs–a church needs to offer each of these settings. If it does not, something will be missing from the Christian community.

Based on how the settings of the church life are structured, and based on their purposes, here is a summary to help you distinguish them:

- The *listening* setting is "hand-to-hand." We wave at one another and shake each other's hands. We are greeted by ushers and they, too, shake our hands.

- The *learning* setting is "face-to-face." Here we see and greet each other up close. We see the teacher and he or she sees us. We are friends who share a Sunday school class.

- The *living* setting is "heart-to-heart." We know each other intimately and we openly learn to share our dreams and desires up close and personally as we develop trust in each other.

These three settings focus on the authority of the Word, interaction with the Word and accountability to the Word respectively.

Let's put it all together ...

Chapter Two:

The Amazing Power of Groups: Some Big Things Small Groups Can Do

*I*n chapter one we learned that small groups are more than some program that's worth adding to your church's already long roster of programs. Small groups are, in fact, a fundamental part of what a church should be about. They are as vital to your life together as worship times and Sunday school classes. So it's not surprising that when churches discover what they've been missing and start a CareRings small group ministry they are amazed at the positive changes small groups bring about in their fellowships. They wonder, *How did we ever get along without CareRings?*

In this chapter we'll highlight some of the specific benefits a CareRings small group ministry can bring to a church and to the individuals within a church. Want your Sunday school and your church to grow in numbers? Start CareRings. Want to hold on to your church's close family atmosphere in the midst of your growth? Start CareRings. Want your people to experience life transformation through applying God's Word in their lives? Start CareRings. Want your people to have a deep personal connection with the Lord through prayer? Start CareRings. Want each person in your church to live every day with a sense of closeness to God? Start CareRings.

Are you catching the theme here? Through CareRing small groups, your church can begin making changes that will make it more what you—and more importantly, God—desire it to be.

GROUPS CAN ENABLE GROWTH TO CONTINUE

When I was serving as associate pastor of First Church of the Nazarene in Nashville, the leaders of a young adult Sunday school class in the church came to me one day and told me their story. They explained that over a period of a few years their class had experienced steady growth and had even moved to a larger classroom. But then, when the class reached about 35 in number, the growth leveled off. They tried a number of approaches to get past this plateau, but to no avail. The class leaders' question to me was: "How can we get the growth trend restarted?"

I probed for some more information about the class. One thing the leaders told me was that the class had begun to use the fourth Sunday of each month to meet in small groups of 10 or 12 around tables during the Sunday school class time. There they discussed the lesson and prayed for each other. This brought some personal attention back into the class, but I could see that it wasn't enough. It was clear to me that the class needed to start real small groups, the kind that meet regularly in homes—CareRings.

We talked at length about the situation, and the leaders agreed to find out more about CareRings. Before long, many of the class's existing small groups began meeting as CareRings in their homes each week (except for the weeks they met as a group in their Sunday school class). Through this approach, the sense of closeness was reborn and the class began to grow again.

That is a real-life example of how, by starting CareRings, a Sunday school class can keep on growing. Many classes have reached a plateau because people intuitively sense that growing larger would cause them to lose any real sense of closeness with one another. CareRings can restore the closeness and allow the class to keep on growing.

But on a larger scale, what about a church that has reached a plateau? There the solution is not quite as simple. But before we look at the situation, let's assess the problem.

> *CareRings can restore the closeness and allow the class to keep on growing.*

Many churches are not growing for some specific reason. Perhaps there are too few seats in the sanctuary, not enough parking spaces, strife or discord within the congregation or an unfriendly attitude among the congregation. These and a hundred other causes can keep a church from reaching its full potential.

External circumstances can also produce a barrier to growth. There could be dramatic ethnic shifts taking place in the local population. Or there could be radical changes in the local economic situation, such as a major plant or factory in a small town closing down. A church has no control over such circumstances, and yet, directly or indirectly, they can affect a church's growth potential.

While we can and should fix the internal circumstances that have caused a church to plateau, there may be nothing we can do about the external causes. But then again, there may even be something we can do in response to external circumstances. In that regard, I'll never forget the story of Pasadena First Church of the Nazarene.

In the mid-1970s a Christian college relocated from Pasadena to San Diego. This caused many of the people in churches around Pasadena to wring their hands in despair, because they had been relying heavily on students, staff and faculty from the college for their support. The prevailing attitude was panic. How would the churches recover from the loss of leadership and membership? Would they even survive?

Interestingly, there was no panic at Pasadena First, even though that church probably stood to lose the most. The pastor, Dr. Earl Lee, prayed and discussed the situation with the church board. They resolved to take action. One thing they chose to do was to hire a full-time pastor of personal evangelism, who trained hundreds of people to share their faith. Another thing they decided to do was to form small groups that would meet in members' homes.

Within less than three years, the church had regained the ground lost by people leaving with the college—and had shown a gain to boot! Most of the other churches in town showed a membership loss for years, and a few of them closed their doors.

What made the difference at Pasadena First? Leadership and a resolve to do what the church should have been doing all along—training members for evangelism and connecting members in small groups.

If small groups can help overcome an external obstacle to growth like key members moving away, how much more can small groups overcome internal problems like discord or unfriendly attitudes? Whether you're looking to get your Sunday school class or your whole church back into a growth mode, small groups can be where the necessary changes take place.

GROUPS CAN KEEP GROWING CHURCHES "SMALL"

A fellow church staff member and friend of mine, Jeffery Johnson, visited Willow Creek Community Church in South Barrington, Illinois for a leadership conference a few years ago. While there, he decided to conduct a personal survey of the Willow Creek laypeople he met. He asked specific questions about the church and its pastor, staff and congregation.

One of those questions was: "What is it you love most about Willow Creek?"

Jeff said the unanimous response he got was: "The most wonderful thing about this church is the closeness of the people. We all feel connected with each other."

This intrigued my friend. You see, the average attendance at Willow Creek in worship is more than 17,000. That hardly sounds like a close, family-like church!

Jeff decided to follow up with another question: "Exactly what is it about the church that makes you feel that way?"

Again he got similar responses from everyone: "It's the small groups. We are close because every week we sit with 10 to 12 people in someone's living room, read the Word, share our joys and sorrows and pray together."

The point is clear—groups keep growing churches "small"! They make the people feel connected with each other. Everyone knows there are a few people they can trust and with who they believe they can share everything. Groups do that. They put people in touch with one another in ways nothing else can.

> *Groups keep growing churches "small"!*

Someone may ask, "Are churches growing because they have groups, or do they have groups because they are growing?" It's a fair question. It might be that churches grow because they keep an atmosphere of smallness through their small groups. Or it might be that they start small groups to meet the needs of a congregation that is growing anyway.

Perhaps both scenarios play out. Or more likely, as churches begin to grow, they are wise enough to see that they cannot keep the same sense of intimacy and closeness they had when they were a smaller fellowship. They design ways of meeting the need for accountability and discipleship training. They discover that they have to develop lay leaders who see care for the spiritual and social aspects of life as part of their responsibility. So partway along a growth curve they start small groups. And, as a result, they grew more!

One church that decided from the start to grow and develop with small groups was New Hope Community Church in Portland, Oregon. Pastor Ray Cotton calls their small groups "TLC groups." Not only do these groups supply their members with tender, loving care but they are also designed to be the setting for outreach and ministry as well as the training of lay pastors. As a result, this dynamic church has grown consistently for 29 years.

In whatever way and at whatever point a church puts small groups in place, the one indispensable element is passion. Passion is intense love for God. Passion is a deep and consistent concern for people, coupled with a clear and strong intent to influence them for Christ and lead them to salvation. Those with passion believe wholeheartedly that reaching others is urgent business and vitally important work. They are deeply broken for the lost and hurting. They focus on finding, caring for and loving everyone who is without God in their lives.

We are far too casual about this high and lofty business of winning others to Christ. It is important to us, but too often it is not urgent. It is not a passion. Small groups offer us a consistent method of naturally building relationships with others and lovingly nudging them toward the Lord.

The small groups at New Hope have worked well in spite of the fact that Oregon is a state where 58 percent of the population claims no religious affiliation. At New Hope, more than 60 percent of new members are also new converts. In the last three decades, this fellowship has grown from zero to more than 3,000 and has built a 2500-seat sanctuary. In fact, they had to go to two worship services the second week they were in the new building. Dr. Carl George says, "New Hope offers one of the best examples of small group ministry in America."[1]

Evangelism, Growth and Small Groups

Almost all churches began small. Few start with as many as 100 people. They typically begin with just a few, perhaps 30 to 50. The difference in their growth seems to depend on a relatively small number of factors.

One is dedication to a vision. If the pastor and people constantly keep their mission before them and maintain enthusiasm for the work, the church tends to grow.

Another factor is the willingness by both the pastor and the people to pay whatever price is necessary to enable the church to grow. This means commitment to the task and a willingness to remove whatever obstacles get between them and others. It means work!

Yet another factor is the quality of spiritual life. In 1989, while doing my doctoral research, I surveyed 2800 people nationwide in all types of evangelical congregations about their spiritual commitment. When I compared the results with those of Dr. Fred Smith (who had earlier gotten his doctorate at Fuller Theological Seminary doing similar research), an amazing fact emerged: people in growing churches are more committed to living a unique Christian lifestyle than those in congregations that are not growing. In fact, of 12 subjects representing spiritual commitment in the survey, commitment to living a truly separated Christian life moved up eight places in growing churches over nongrowing fellowships.[2]

> *Big churches are small churches that began fulfilling the Great Commission.*

Big churches are small churches that began fulfilling the Great Commission. They "go," they "teach," they "baptize" and they "preach" the Good News. Their people have found that it is fun to win another person to Jesus that their lives are literally filled with effort to find and influence the "lost."

When churches grow rapidly, when they get far too big for the pastor and staff to care for the needs, small groups keep people in contact with each other. Again, they empower and organize the laity to serve and provide ministry. Growing churches can stay small with groups. They need never lose the sense of family.

Holding on to the Family Atmosphere

People in growing churches understand that others are not automatically going to heaven just because they prayed the "sinner's prayer." They know that the Master's mandate is that we "make disciples"—and that means more than just conversion. While Matthew 28:19–20 includes the going, the teaching, the baptizing and so on, the focus of these verses is making disciples. In fact, "make disciples" is the only command in those verses; it alone is in the imperative mood.

We should keep our attention on the process of making disciples, since this is a part of the evangelistic work we are to perform. It is not another work, but it is part and parcel of the whole work of bringing people to Christ and getting them into heaven.

To do this, we must stay close to our people. We must find ways to know them—really know them—in significant relationships and in comfortable, natural settings. It will take time (lots of it!) to know them and for them to know us at this level.

One significant element is some means for the congregation to provide quality care—physically, emotionally and spiritually—for its people. Sounds like small groups, doesn't it? There are many means, but by far the most effective is small groups.

GROUPS CAN HELP US APPLY THE SCRIPTURES

No preacher or Sunday school teacher worthy of the position is concerned only with conveying biblical information. They want those listening to the sermon or the lesson not only to know what the Bible says but also to put into practice what it *means* for those listening. They want their listeners to understand *and* apply the Scriptures.

Nevertheless, the worship service and the Sunday school class are both relatively formal settings where you can get away with just gathering information if you want to. Not so with a small group. A small group is such an intimate setting that you can't ignore application of the Scriptures even if you wanted to. You're talking about the Bible with a few people who know you really well. You've *got* to consider how Joseph's uprightness sheds light on your temptation. You've *got* to think about what Jesus' teaching on loving enemies says about your relationship with that mean coworker of yours.

In short, small groups are a great place to learn how to apply God's teaching to the realities of your everyday life. And two major areas where they help their members apply Scripture are, first of all, in breaking through legalistic traditions to embrace the love of God, and, second of all, in helping people get over their regrets about the past and their worries about the future.

Changing Your "Should" to "Could" and Your "Ought" to "Can"

Many Christians grew up in churches where the evidence of salvation was adherence to rules or regulations. They were told, explicitly or implicitly, that the evidence of holiness was how you dressed, how you wore your hair or makeup, or where you went or didn't go. And so they were raised with a mental image of God standing on the edge of heaven, arms folded, forehead furrowed with a scowl, waiting to see if they would follow the rules. As a result, they concluded that God's approval and love hinged on their doing or not doing whatever their tradition told them was embodied in the "code." They came to trust their behavior rather than God and to put faith in their works instead of his grace. So they came away with a set of "shoulds" and "oughts," believing that, if they strictly adhered to the list, they would be okay.

> They came to trust their behavior rather than God and to put faith in their works instead of his grace.

There are two problems with this scenario.

The first is that it produced a few generations of people who observed exterior Christianity only. It showed up in their teaching, preaching and living. Some subjects were seldom mentioned, while others were openly attacked. It sounded as though you could be greedy as long as you didn't gamble. You could be self-righteous, just not "selfish." Many who didn't cuss were inwardly covetous. Others who wouldn't go drinking in public were dogmatic and demanding in private.

The second problem is that this view produced people who were sensitive to what they "ought" to do but hardly noticed how they could love God and others. How they "should" live overshadowed what they could be. What God wanted them to do or where he wanted them to go seemed to mean more than what they could become by his grace. So the whole idea of Christianity drifted into a form of legalism.

How brash of us to feel that any shred of our behavior could in any way be the means of righteousness! What idolatry for us to self-righteously believe anything we do could cause God to love us more! How wrong of us to believe that whatever we didn't do could cause him to love us less! That's where it breaks down. God's love is an absolute. He doesn't love us "because." He just loves us!

> God's love is an absolute. He doesn't love us "because." He just loves us!

As people sit together week after week under the guidance of a trained leader, carefully pouring over the Word and praying for guidance, some of these misconceptions will surface. When we honor God's Word, he honors us. Something about the interchange and dialogue, something about becoming vulnerable and trusting, fosters openness, brokenness—and oneness. By God's grace, he works us through the old barriers and breaks us through to new levels of love and obedience.

In a supportive atmosphere of groups, the Scripture is opened and we allow God's Spirit to witness with our spirit. He confirms in us what we have heard, taught and preached. We come to believe it more because we have had an active part in opening it, praying over it and discovering its richness and deep authority.

Dealing with Your "If Only's" and Your "What If's"

Few people are free from failings and fears. The failings of the past and fears about the future inhibit, intimidate and sometimes even tyrannize us. We can get caught up in the "if only's"—regrets over past mistakes, failures and sins. Others of us are paralyzed by fears of the future—the "what if's."

A friend of mine, Jack Eyestone, used to say, "There are only two things you shouldn't worry about. One is the things you can't do anything about. No amount of fretting will change them. The other is the things you *can* do something about. Worry won't change them either—only work will. So get to work!"

The past and the future, the "if only's" and the "what if's," too often bother us. If we let them, they will keep us from even trying to get things accomplished. They will nag at us and threaten our effectiveness.

As we open the Word week after week, small groups provide a setting in which the powerful stories of the living Word come to life before our eyes. We see that men such as Noah, Moses, David and Paul had sinned—grievously sinned—and yet overcame it by the love and grace of God. We see the fear of the future melt away in Stephen, who blessed others as he was being stoned.

We've heard these stories preached year after year. How can they come to life anymore in small groups? The answer lies in our personal involvement with the Word in small groups.

Twenty-first-century American Christians are lazy! We live on the watered-down milk of another person's study when we read a book, listen to a Sunday school lesson or hear a message

> *We live on the watered-down milk of another person's study when we read a book, listen to a Sunday school lesson or hear a message preached—unless we act on it.*

preached—unless we act on it. And many of us don't. We listen, agree and go on.

For the tide to turn, there has to be a new gravitational force that pulls us into the Holy Bible for answers again. We have got to become men and women of the Word. We have to encounter the Scriptures for ourselves in a small group made up of people who know us and love us and want us to become more like our Savior.

GROUPS CAN HELP US HAVE A MEANINGFUL PRAYER LIFE

Since the church is the body of Christ, there is a close and vital relationship between Christ and the Christian community. And the most natural way to think of the relationship between the head and members of the body is in terms of the nerves. In the physical body, nerves carry messages from the members to the head with reports of touch, smell, sight, hearing and taste. Similarly, the head gives signals to the members to move, turn, touch, smell and so on. There is constant communication between the two, with hundreds of messages going out every one-thousandth of a second.

When this communication is not working properly, we experience a physical condition called disease. Nervous disorders can show themselves in one of two ways. First, impaired movement includes a whole spectrum of illnesses in which the parts of the body do not carry out whatever orders the mind gives them. Second, a whole other set of diseases shows up in symptoms of numbness, loss of sight, loss of hearing and so on. In these two ways, then, communication breaks down, whether in the sensory or muscular functions of the nervous system.

Prayer is the nervous system of the spiritual body. It is therefore the link between us and God. And prayer should include both kinds of messages—sensory and muscular.

We all understand the "sensory" part. Here we give God messages. We tell him what we need, we pray for others and we give God praise and thanksgiving. There's nothing wrong with

> *Prayer is the nervous system of the spiritual body. ... the link between us and God.*

this part of prayer. But for some of us, it can degenerate into talking *to* God instead of talking *with* him.

The other part is the "muscular" part of prayer in which the Godhead sends the message to the body. In this part of prayer we listen to God. We sense what is of value and importance to him and pray about it or act according to his guidance. This form is often overlooked or ignored. Certainly, I have made far too little time in my prayer life for responsive listening to God. Yet we have his word, "Be still, and know that I am God" (Ps. 46:10). Sometimes I imagine that, if God weren't such a gentleman, he would say, "Will you please shut up and let me get a few words in? Please just stop all your living and laughing so you can listen to me."

True prayer is both speaking to God and listening to him speak. CareRings help us develop the practice of true prayer.

The Place of Prayer in Worship and Small Groups

In most worship services we pray together. However, all too often this means listening to and agreeing with someone else (typically the pastor) who verbalizes prayers for us. The only weakness in this approach is that our minds tend to wander during prayers spoken by another. There is a vast difference between listening to a prayer and actually praying!

Prayer in worship is fundamental and indispensable. It is a community event in which the pastor and the people gather around concerns and needs shared by the entire fellowship. It makes the statement that we do not serve God alone; we are all a part of the others, and we have a responsibility to them. Yet we do not normally make more of such prayers than that. We cannot take time to hear many needs and share them up close and personal. In this regard, small groups offer this intimate dimension of prayer unavailable to us in the celebration setting of worship.

We must enable all Christians to pray personally and intimately about their own and a few others' concerns. The place for that kind of prayer is small groups.

The Power of Prayer

In college, years ago, I first heard of Rosalind Rinker and her books on prayer, including *Prayer and Teaching Conversational Prayer.* In her books I discovered two principles that I have never forgotten. I have seen both of them work wonders in CareRings.

- *Pray faith-sized prayers.* Many people pray prayers they don't believe God will answer even as they pray them. They may give intellectual assent to the idea that God answers prayer. Yet all too often they pray for things they don't truly believe God will—or even can—provide. There is questioning in their minds and doubting in their hearts as they pray for a lost friend or a financial need.

One illustration of Rinker's is about a man who had a new neighbor move in next door. The man had been thinking about being a witness, so he began to pray for the new neighbor. As he did, he noticed that he was only *saying* prayers, not really *believing* them in his heart. He was alarmed. So he prayed that God would show him the way to pray for his neighbor and believe.

He thought, *What prayer could I pray for my neighbor that I would actually believe God could and would answer?* He hit on the idea of praying that the Lord would give him an opportunity to visit with his friend. As he prayed, he knew in his heart that he truly believed God would answer. He began actively looking for God to give him the chance, and within a week God answered his prayer. He was mowing his lawn one Saturday morning while his neighbor was working in his yard. They introduced themselves to one another and visited for a while. I'll call the neighbor Bill.

God had answered his prayer. The man's faith grew stronger.

Then he thought, *What prayer can I pray next?* He asked the Lord to show him something the neighbor liked that the two might have in common so that they could spend some time together. Again, within a matter of days, as they got to know each other better he soon found out that the neighbor loved football.

You guessed it. His next prayer was "Lord, I need a couple of football tickets so Bill and I can build a relationship." He was not ready for what happened next. The next day at his job a coworker announced he had a couple of tickets to a pro football game to give away. The man jumped on the offer. When he invited his new neighbor, Bill said he was free on that date and would love to go to the game.

Again, the Christian's faith grew stronger as he became convinced that God truly wanted to save Bill.

As he got ready for the game he prayed that the conversation would open into some topic of spiritual importance so he could share Christ with Bill. Later, on the way home from the game, Bill began talking about his problems and said, "I don't know where to turn. Everybody has advice, but I need someone who really knows what is best." And with that, the witnessing began as this man told Bill how God had made a difference for him and his family.

Bill accepted Christ as his Savior within a few weeks.[3]

Now, that is the power of faith-sized prayers, and that's how we pray in CareRings. Since we are together week after week, we can bring our concerns, progress reports and current needs to a group of trusted friends whom we literally hear calling out to God with us for our concerns.

- *Pray freely and conversationally.* Prayer isn't something you do just because you think you're supposed to. It's something you should do because you want to, because you have things on your heart that you want to tell God. So prayer must be genuine and heartfelt.

That's why one firm guideline in CareRings is that no one be put on the spot by being asked to pray aloud in the group. Some people are very self-conscious about praying before others. It's not unheard of that a new small group member has left the group because of embarrassment over being forced to pray out loud. Out of respect to the members of a group, praying in a CareRing is something you are expected to do only if you want to.

> *Prayer isn't something you do just because you think you're supposed to. It's something you should do because you want to.*

Another guideline in CareRings is that prayer should involve praying naturally, whenever you feel led to and using normal, casual speech. In the CareRing ministry where I pastor, we saw the power of this aspect of prayer dialogue dramatically lived out not long ago. At a monthly leaders' meeting, Jim and Bev told the story of Carolee, who had been in their group for more than two years and had never once prayed.

After Jim shared about conversational prayer—just talking with the Lord—the CareRing began praying and Carolee opened her mouth and prayed for the first time in the group. The other CareRing members were taken aback, but it brought them a joy that they are still talking about. That's the power of natural, conversational prayer.

Prayer and Relationships

Think back to our comparison of prayer to the human nervous system. That comparison showed how prayer maintains our relationship with God. For the relationship to be healthy, there needs to be interchange between the body and mind, between us and God.

But there is another relationship that prayer can help us to maintain. It is our relationship with other people. Sometimes this kind of relationship is called a horizontal relationship, while our relationship with God is called a vertical one.

The cross symbolizes both of these dimensions. With his head near God and his feet near earth, Jesus Christ bridged the age-old gulf between God and sinners. He became a sacrifice for sins because he lived and died a real man. But his arms were also stretched out toward others. We hear him touching another's life even as he hung on the cross. One of the thieves asked for forgiveness and Jesus promised, "Today you will be with me in paradise" (Luke 23:43).

The vertical dimension is a relationship between us and God. An open, active relationship with God is essential to an effective Christian experience. As the Christmas song says, "God and sinners reconciled ... ." It is vitally important that our relationship with God be given careful attention and that we assist one another to take care in this area. Prayer within CareRings is a great way to accomplish this goal.

The horizontal dimension is a relationship between ourselves and other Christians. This relationship between ourselves and others is also maintained through honest and open prayer. If prayer involves listening to God and being sensitive to him and his will, then we can expect to receive urgings or promptings from God about our relationships with, and attitudes toward others. What better place to openly admit needs in our lives and to lovingly support others in their needs during prayer times than in a small group?

Prayer Dialogue

There is no relationship among humans that does not involve dialogue. We build relationships with friends through conversation. We develop relationships with coworkers in formal communication and informal discussion. Dialogue is the interaction, and communication that is interchanged between us and others. We share ideas, stories, needs, dreams, hopes and fears, and the others do the same. There is an exchange of lives in dialogue.

What is prayer dialogue? It is interacting with God and one another. It is shared praying. In CareRings we guide people into this higher level of openness before God and one another. It need not be forced. No one has to "make it happen." But it will happen! Give God's people an opportunity to open themselves up before God in a supportive and loving atmosphere, and then stand back! God will respond to your searching, and you will discover a reality about his presence you have seldom known. Prayer dialogue is community with and before God.

> *What is prayer dialogue? It is interacting with God and one another. It is shared praying.*

As in any productive personal conversation, prayer needs to be a common effort to build a relationship. It needs to be regulated by acceptable rules and guidelines of ordinary conversation. Basic "rules" of prayer dialogue, therefore, include the following:

- ***Participants should listen to God as well as speak to him.*** Since prayer dialogue is an offering up of needs, thanksgiving and praise to the Father, we allow him time to speak back to us. In fact, in prayer dialogue we intentionally remain open to his prompting, and consequently we do not become nervous when no one is praying.

- ***No one should dominate the prayer time.*** We take turns praying, and we pray no more than two to three sentences at a time. It is simply not polite for someone to interrupt others when they are praying or to control the time spent together.

- ***No one should presume to pray on behalf of the whole group.*** It is wrong to speak for others in their presence. Therefore, we use first person pronouns—*I, me, my* and so on—when we speak to God in prayer.

- ***Everyone may pray as often as they like.*** Healthy conversation involves all the participants, each listening when others are speaking and all making contributions freely. So it's okay when someone prays more than once.

- ***Each person should pay attention to the others' prayers.*** While an individual is praying, the others should be actively listening and agreeing with the prayer in their spirits. This unites all together in the prayer being lifted up to God.

- ***Prayers should use normal, conversational language.*** There may be a place for prayer using the "thees" and "thous" of King James language, but a CareRing is not it. Here we try to impress no one and take the feelings and understanding level of others into account.

GROUPS CAN BRING BACK THE CLOSENESS

A dear friend of mine, Gary Haines, sings a wonderful song entitled "Bring Back the New Again." It is a prayer that God will renew his presence and joy in our lives. It is a call to God for him to bring back the thrill and passion as it once was. That song moves my heart toward God every time I hear Gary sing it. It stirs a longing I have to know God and be known by him.

I believe this longing resides in every human heart. Perhaps, in some long, dark winter of the soul, it may lie dormant for years. But it is there nevertheless.

One thing small groups can do is revitalize individuals spiritually and sensitize them toward God. This can happen in at least two ways.

- ***Small groups can break down barriers between us and God.*** We've talked about the "if only's" and the "what if's." There are some walls between us and God that have to do more with our reaction to what has happened to us in the past or with what we fear about the future than with the events, problems or circumstances themselves.

It is one thing to be abused and another to resent or hate the one who abused you. It is one thing to be taken advantage of and another to retaliate against the one who took advantage. It is one thing to be used or hurt and another to be bitter, indignant or hostile. The first is hurtful, even lamentable. The second—our response to what happened—is poisonous to ourselves and destructive of others. We must forgive the first and be forgiven of the second.

Only when both God and we are forgiving can there be oneness. God is always forgiving, but it can take us a while to sense it. And it can take even longer for us to be forgiving. If we will not forgive, there is no forgiveness for us (Matt. 6:14-15; 18:21-35; Mark 11:25), so this is truly an important issue.

> *If we will not forgive, there is no forgiveness for us.*

If there is surface forgiveness only, leaving deeper resentment or bitterness, that is a barrier between us and God. Of course, it can be removed by his grace. But to come to the place where we allow him to do that takes time, love and support from those around us.

- **Small groups can get us back to essentials.** As a young pastor in El Paso, Texas, I went through some difficult times. Those were wonderful days in many ways, and I was fortunate to have some truly remarkable people in our congregation. But for me, it was an unsettling time. I went there to pastor the largest church of our denomination in the city, and I got caught up in the responsibilities of my position and the needs and problems within the church.

Dealing with those concerns became my primary task. As you might imagine, the needs and my attempt to "solve the problems" became a preoccupation. The result? I became frustrated and irritated, even to the point of taking it out on some of those precious people.

Finally, in desperation, I began to call out to God for help. It was some time before I got through—not because of his resistance but because of my close-mindedness. You see, I hadn't caused the problems in our church; others had. And so God had to deal with them. Or so I thought!

In all this turmoil, I was driving home one afternoon, listening to a new tape by Bill and Gloria Gaither. They were singing a song I had never heard before entitled "More of You." The message went, "Of things I've had my fill, and yet I hunger still. Empty and bare, Lord, hear my prayer for more of you."

That's all it took. As I listened to the words, God started speaking to me. My eyes filled with tears, I pulled my car to the side of the freeway, folded my arms over the steering wheel, lowered my head and cried out my soul to God, begging forgiveness. "More of you. Of things I've had my fill, and yet I hunger still ... ." It was breakthrough time! It is still a blessing to me now as I relate the story.

What happened? I got back to essentials. Now it was no longer God blessing my work; it was me trying to help in his work. I was not asking for his help (although I did that), but I was asking, "How can I help you today, God? What can I do for you? What do you want me to preach?" He was no longer my servant upon whom I called for help. I became his servant. I willingly took orders from the Lord. That very same work that had been frustrating and irritating became a joy!

> *It was no longer God blessing my work; it was me trying to help in his work.*

Can you relate to what I'm talking about? Perhaps you are in a position of turmoil right now. I was alone in the car when God took me back to essentials and restored the sense of closeness I'd once had with him. But how much sooner might I have known such release if I'd been sharing my problems in a small group? You can get back your closeness with God—as well as experience other practical benefits—in a CareRing with people who love you. Unleash the amazing power of small groups in your church.

Chapter Three:

CareRings in Context: Welcome to the Wonderful World of Small Groups

It's an exciting time when the leaders of a local church are beginning to plan how to put small groups into place in their church. But in a way, I can't help feeling sorry for them, too. They are faced with a bewildering array of competing theories and contradictory approaches. The list of options appears endless. It can feel a little like going to a restaurant and being handed a menu the size of New York City's yellow pages. How can they choose a single dish from such a huge menu?

This chapter is an attempt to make things easier by providing a broad view of the small group landscape. Here you'll learn the primary models that most small groups fall into. You'll also run down a list of basic types of small groups. At the end of it all, the small group options should appear much less bewildering.

Another thing this chapter will accomplish is to help you understand how CareRings fit into the overall picture of what small group ministry is all about. Of course, CareRings—those small groups designed to complement a church's existing adult education program—are not necessarily the only small groups your church needs. So this chapter provides you with some food for thought as you consider CareRings as one key part of your church's total approach to small groups.

Now, let's get started exploring the wonderful world of small groups!

THREE PRIMARY SMALL GROUP MODELS

There are literally dozens of books and manuals for small groups put out by publishers in the U.S. every year. A search on the Internet turns up innumerable resources about small groups. Hundreds of churches and parachurch organizations offer some form of seminar or conference to teach others about small groups. Is there any way to make sense of it all? Yes, there is. Despite the proliferation of information about small groups, most of what is out there can be grouped into three primary schools of thought or models for doing small group ministry: the metachurch model, the cell church model and "publisher models."

The Metachurch Model

For many years, Carl George served as a pastor in Florida. Later, while a professor at Fuller Theological Seminary, he identified a movement among churches that he later termed "metachurches." His concept of huddles, district coaches and leaders are all carefully developed in his book *Prepare Your Church for the Future* (Revell, 1991) and in his other writings about the metachurch model.

Carl George developed this model to refer to large congregations that are broken down into small groups. Each small group is a little "church," whereas the whole body is the "metachurch." (The prefix *meta-* means "above" or "beyond.")

George and other proponents of the metachurch model believe community is a primary and essential part of Christian life. So in a metachurch, everyone who is involved in any ministry within the fellowship is in a small group for creating community. Indeed, everyone who is connected with the metachurch is encouraged to be part of a small group.

The metachurch model tends to be especially popular in megachurches. And, in fact, at America's largest church—Willow Creek Community Church in South Barrington, Illinois—pastors such as Bill Donahue and Russ Robinson have honed one of the nation's most significant small group ministries using the metachurch model. As one spends time visiting with those men, and with other leaders at Willow

Creek, you begin to see the long shadow of theologian Gilbert Bilezikian and practical theorist Carl George.

At Willow Creek, for instance, there are task groups, children's groups, seekers' groups and groups for adults of every age grouping. In the year 2000 a remarkable thing happened there. While the church averaged 17,100 per weekend in worship events, their average meeting weekly in small groups was 17,300! Obviously, a major force in the development of that church in recent years has been small groups.

The Cell Church Model

The cell church model bears some resemblance to the metachurch model, but it has a different history and maintains some different emphasis.

The idea originated—or at least was popularized—by Paul Yonggi Cho of Seoul, South Korea, and by Dale Galloway at New Hope Community Church in Portland, Oregon. One of the earliest leaders to conceptualize how groups would fit within the whole church setting was Peter Wagner, who often taught about "celebration," "congregation," and "cell," the three spheres of activity in the healthy church. Today Ralph W. Neighbour Jr. is perhaps the primary leader of the cell church movement through his TOUCH Ministries.

The primary and distinctive idea of the cell church model is that everyone who is part of the church is in a small group or "cell." The basic or foundational settings of church involvement are worship and small group life. The concept is that every living thing God created grows by cell multiplication, and so should the church. If everyone is in a cell, then everyone is connecting with others and is directly involved.

The weakness with the cell church model is that little, if any, value is placed on teaching. While there is mention of teaching within the worship setting in cell literature, it soon becomes obvious that teaching is not a primary concern of the movement.

Publisher Models

Plans and approaches that are published by Serendipity House, NavPress and Pilgrimage Press, among others, can be grouped under the broad classification "publisher models." At last count, well over two dozen publishers have some form or system of small group ministry material available. While they do not advocate, or even agree on, one particular approach, they do provide excellent resources and offer both curriculum and organizational ideas that can be adapted for use in any local church.

The advantage in these resources is that leaders can pick and choose the materials that fit them best. They might select curriculum from one publisher and adopt the structure and nomenclature of another. Using published curriculum, they are less likely to try to import a program into their church and impose someone else's ministry upon their people.

A weakness in this model is that these publishers have to rely on field practitioners who may not be saying the same things to those they advise or train. This can result in confusion for leaders in the local church. Still, field practitioners typically are effective leaders of local ministries who have wide and successful experience building small group ministries.

TYPES OF SMALL GROUPS

There are many different types of groups in local churches, and we'll discuss several of the most common types shortly. But at the outset, I want to underscore the importance of church leaders learning to appreciate the value that each of these kinds of groups can offer a church. Leaders should avoid the temptation of thinking that one type of small group—usually a type they have tried and found useful—is where it's at and that all the others are inferior. Churches are better off when they use a carefully selected combination of types of small groups.

One church I visited uses only task-oriented groups (those in which the ministry or service includes a group time). They appear blind to the option of outreach or seeker groups. Task groups have worked for them, and so they seem to have concluded that the only effective groups are task groups. In reality, quite the opposite is true. Every one of the types of groups discussed in this section has its value and fills an important role in Christian community. In fact, we use most of these in the CareRing ministry. Most are still related to the adult Sunday school, but some work with other departments; such as youth, music or men's/women's ministry.

As you read about the different types, take note of the wide variety of personalities they have, each with its purpose and sense of divine appointment in God's plan for evangelism, building community and sharing gifts.

"Generic Groups": Built on a Balance of Purposes

"Generic groups" are those with a balanced approach to ministry. They have no single, unique function to perform. These groups typically combine prayer and spiritual edification, Bible study and application and caregiving. These groups may be called something like "TLC groups" (tender loving care) or "neighborhood groups" or "home groups," but that differs from church to church.

CareRings are one version of "generic groups." CareRings do not have a specialized function or focus but rather serve the broad purposes of application, fellowship and prayer. What makes them unique is not what occurs during their meeting times but the fact that they are coordinated with the adult Sunday school.

"Generic groups," like CareRings, are among the most popular in churches today. One reason may be that "generic groups" fit well in the traditional church. While transforming a traditional congregation into a small group fellowship can be a major undertaking, "generic groups" are relatively easy for people to understand and join because they serve the functions that people normally think of as "church activities."

Special-Interest Groups: Built on Concern About a Topic

Human nature, being what it is, causes many people to see something as important only when it relates to them personally. We call this connection a person's "felt need." These are the concerns or interests of which they are aware.

When a parent has a discipline problem with his or her child, that's a need in the eyes of that person. The real need may *not* be lack of discipline within the child but rather a lack of leadership on the part of the parent. Likewise, many of us see a difficult relationship with another person as the "problem," whereas in reality the problem may be the effect of something deeper and internal to ourselves, like jealousy, resentment or selfishness. Therefore, to solve the problem that has been identified, we often need to go deeper. To help discipline the child, we need to teach the parent responsible parenting. To improve the relationship, we need to deal with the jealousy, resentment or selfishness.

Though the real needs may be deeper and more intricate than an individual knows, the only way to help them discover the real need may be to attract them through the study of some topic or felt need. Special-interest groups appeal to people on the basis of commonly identified concerns. Then, hopefully, the group can help people go deeper into their own lives to find and deal with more significant problems.

I have seen topical groups of all descriptions. There are the groups for those with aging parents, for parents of middle schoolers, for the recently divorced, for veterans, for Gen Xers, for the blind, for those who have lost a child. The list goes on ... And why not? Why not try to reach every available person through every possible means? Topical groups do just that. The content of the studies is focused on that need and how to cope. As the lessons progress from the simple to the more complex, group members begin to deal with their hurt, their loss, their inner attitudes and biases.

Special-interest groups are an excellent tool to reach someone who would not attend a "generic" group. Many people have to know the purpose being served by their time in the small group. Others are hurting so badly that they do not believe they are ready for an "ordinary" group. And some are so overwhelmed with that particular concern that they are highly motivated to find help and support.

Support Groups: Built on a Need or Hurt

Literally thousands of people who sit within the walls of our churches each week in worship are hurting. They suffer from severe financial problems, from strife within their families, from the loss of a loved one, from divorce and from a dozen other pressures and pains.

Support groups are designed specifically to meet the needs of these precious people. Patterned after Alcoholics Anonymous, support groups typically meet weekly, often at the church. They may be ongoing, or they may meet for a stated number of weeks or months. They differ from special-interest groups in that the participants know what their real need is and are dealing with it through a 12-Step or similar program.

Many times the leaders are people who have a deep concern for the hurt their people are feeling, and many of them have been through similar trauma or trials as their group members. In Alcoholics Anonymous these leaders might be called the "sponsors." They make excellent leaders because they have experienced the loss, the hurt and the embarrassment their people have, and they know from experience that it is neither wise nor helpful to the health of their group members to allow them to wallow in self-pity or remorse.

A few examples of support groups include Divorce Recovery, Weigh Down Workshops, Parents of Eighth Graders (boy, do *they* need our prayers!), and People With Aging Parents. Support groups are one of the best ways to get people started in small groups. They meet urgent needs and can enable people to see that groups are not painful or threatening settings.

Cell Groups: Built on Worship and Giftedness

Cell groups are unique in that they fit into the cell church setting. These congregations are made up of cells, and every person in the fellowship is invited and expected to be part of one. They normally meet weekly for prayer, fellowship and mutual ministry. In fact, ordinarily all local and missionary ministry is performed through the cell structure.

There are hundreds of cell churches in America today. Ralph W. Neighbour's organization publishes the periodical *Cell Groups* and leads seminars and conferences nationally to help them.

One of the most common models for planting new churches today is the cell church model. Perhaps this is true because transforming a traditional church into the cell church model may be more than a congregation can undertake effectively. Also, when a church is started from ground zero, it is easy to bring people into the cell and congregational setting where there is little or no educational ministry in place.

Covenant Groups: Built on a Promise

Covenant groups form with specific goals that the group aims to reach within a matter of time. They meet for the express purpose of mutual edification, accountability and spiritual maturity, rather than focusing on a specific need or concern. The agreement signed by all leaders and members at the beginning is renewable at the point where the group fulfills its initial term of meetings. The most common term is one year, though some agree to meet for six or nine months.

The commitment people are asked to make to the ministry is both its strength and its weakness. Positively, the commitment gives each member a profound sense of ownership in the ministry. Negatively, if a member decides to quit for some reason, he or she is generally asked to explain to the group the reason for that decision. And then that person's having signed a covenant and broken it can lead to a sense of guilt or failure.

Yet many congregations have used the covenant group approach successfully for years. The approach seems to work especially well in old-line churches that are well established, with years of tradition.

Discipleship Groups: Built on Accountability

A form of small group ministry that has not caught on as a national trend, and yet one that is very valuable, is discipleship groups. Often called "accountability groups," discipleship groups are typically made up of one leader (the discipler) and one or two persons being discipled. (For lack of a better term, we call these people the "disciplees.") To easily identify with each other's feelings, needs and views, it is important that both the discipler and the ones being discipled are of the same gender.

Discipleship groups are more than what Barry Woodbridge calls "spiritual friends."[1] They are also less intense than "spiritual direction"—a term commonly employed in the Roman Catholic community.

The discipler is neither a casual "big spiritual brother" nor a know-it-all guru. He or she is neither the answer person nor just a buddy and fellow traveler. Disciplers are guides and encouragers who extend caution, challenges or even warnings—all in an atmosphere of support and love. Sometimes the discipler is called the "mentor." This is fine as long as the term does not carry the connotation of giving directions and being the "super saint."

Discipleship groups meet once a week, typically for an hour. The objective of their time together is for the discipler to lead the disciplee to become a fully devoted follower of Jesus in every area of life. Therefore, the times they have together are less social and always include some form of accountability. Hopefully, within a year or so, the disciplee is ready to be trained and to take on someone else to disciple.

In my church we have found discipleship groups to be an excellent method of moving a young, growing Christian on rapidly in his or her experience with the Lord. We provide a wide variety of materials the discipler may choose from, depending on the maturity and ability of the one being discipled.

We've discovered that the more clearly the discipler enters into the growing and learning experience alongside the disciplee, the sooner and more probable it is that the new Christian will move along to disciple someone else.

Seeker Groups: Built on Evangelism

Jim, a member of our congregation, is one of the most effective witnesses I have ever met. He has led literally hundreds of people to the Lord. Every week of the year, Jim comes in contact with someone who needs Christ. Jim asks if the person wants to pray for salvation—nearly always he or she does—and so another person is led to the Lord.

Jim would say he just does what God put in his heart to do—serve God completely. The first transformation in his life happened when he accepted Christ as his personal Savior. But there was another change. Jim also came to a place where he dedicated everything he is to the Lord. He is a businessman who, along with Bev, his wife, has built quite a business. Yet Jim would be quick to tell you that their business success is nothing compared with the joy of praying with someone who wants to turn his or her life over to God.

He teaches an adult education class for new believers, many of whom he has led to the Lord himself. Out of that class have come CareRings of new converts and groups for seekers. Hardly a week goes by that someone does not come to God because of a call or conversation Jim has had with that person.

This is just one example of a seeker group. These are small groups started by people with a passion and gift for evangelism who want to get into their communities and neighborhoods with the Gospel of Christ. You might call them "marketplace evangelists." They go where the people are. They love them just as they are and win them to the Lord. Groups that are started with the stated purpose of winning others to the Lord are seeker groups. We need more of them.

Gated communities and apartment complexes today offer ideal settings in which to form such groups. The reason God led one Christian to such a home environment may be because, as an insider with the key or gate combination, he or she is the ideal person to start a Bible study in that community.

Sunday School Groups: Built on Christian Education

One of the most powerful and effective approaches I have seen using small groups within the Sunday school is at Flamingo Road Community Church in Fort Lauderdale, Florida. There, every adult education class is arranged with groups of eight chairs in horseshoe shapes with the open end toward the front of the class. Teachers are trained in leading small groups and are taught how to facilitate discussion. This is important, because many teachers of adults know only the lecture method of instruction and have focused on creative approaches or innovative methods. They need to be retrained in small group dynamics if an adult education ministry attempts to transition to this format.

There are two significant advantages this approach offers: (1) No one is asked to come a second time to church or to a home for a small group meeting to get a quality small group experience; (2) The adult education class becomes a center of fellowship and interaction with other members.

There are also some drawbacks in the approach. Since the Sunday school hour is used, interaction is limited by time. Also, good teachers do not necessarily make good small group leaders. It is essential that only teachers who can make the transition be used with this approach. If not, they will either stifle discussion or class time will be filled with the pooling of students' unformed ideas. Then, too, there is an authentic concern for biblical content. It is an unusual teacher who can get *both* quality Bible content across *and* enable the small groups in his or her class to interact with one another deeply.

Sunday school groups differ from CareRings in that they meet in the classroom during Sunday school time, while CareRings (though made up primarily of Sunday school class members) meet in homes during the week. Of course, they can be combined.

Kids' Groups: Built on Children's and Youth Ministries

Grown-ups are not the only ones to benefit from meeting regularly with a few other Christians. Children and youth also open up more and draw closer in small groups. Building on existing children's and youth ministries, a church can meet the need for close fellowship among its young people. In my church, for example, we have GAP (Going After the Power) groups for middle schoolers and Rock groups for high schoolers.

The GAP groups are groups of from six to eight students in the sixth through eighth grades who meet following a combined time with the whole youth department on Wednesday nights.

Since high school students either own their own cars or have friends who do, Rock groups are held on a night other than Wednesday. Rock groups are student led, but each group has an adult individual or couple sponsoring it. They use the same material as the middle schoolers, but it has been modified to fit the more mature high school students.

Even children below middle school love to get together in small groups. For example, many Sunday school classes for kids have incorporated a "break-out time" when kids gather with an adult in a group of about half a dozen for study and discussion. Methods like these help young people grow accustomed to the small group experiences they'll have later in life.

Work Groups: Built on a Helpful Project

Building a house for a low income family through the local branch of Habitat for Humanity. Spending ten days in Haiti building a clinic where missionary doctors will dispense the hope of the Gospel along with their medicines. These are just a couple of examples of what small groups from churches can do to serve others while growing closer to one another and to God.

Work groups are often temporary but intense kinds of small groups. There may be a preparation period of Bible study, followed by the actual work project. During the work project itself, some time is often set aside for devotions or prayer. Maybe during a work project like the clinic-building project in Haiti, group members will take time out to evangelize the locals. Afterward, a time of celebration is in order.

Work groups can often be tremendously bonding and growing experiences for their members. They can be fulfilling, too, as members come to know the joy of giving to others in Christlike unselfishness.

Ministry Groups: Built on Serving Teams

Some Christians have become so busy doing good things in the church that they have little or no time for God. Ministry team groups are founded on the principle that absolutely everyone needs community, maturity and significant spiritual experiences, including those who are already serving in the church in some capacity. Perhaps *especially* including those people.

I have found that just because people are involved in serving in a church's ministry does *not* mean they automatically feel they are a part of the church and that they belong. Also, I have seen all too many committed, dedicated workers become burned out when there was no personal interaction with others over the Word.

What if, in every ministry team of the church (youth workers, women's ministry leaders, whatever), every participant was involved in a weekly time dedicated to reflection and spiritual exercises? What if, as a part of what they regularly do—whether singing in the praise team, leading the youth group or teaching a children's Sunday school class—everyone spent at least thirty minutes of quality time each week with others with whom they serve? I believe the burnout rate would go down. I suspect they would all feel even more that they belonged. I am sure they would stay longer at the church and be more fulfilled. That's why we need ministry small groups.

The timing for ministry groups can differ. These groups can meet in conjunction with the ministry itself, such as greeters and ushers gathering for half an hour before their duties at a worship service. (Sometimes, in such a case, the group is called a "task group.") Or a ministry team can meet in their "off time" at someone's home during the week. For example, all the children's Sunday school teachers could meet in the home of the Sunday school superintendent on Saturday night.

Perhaps the setting most commonly overlooked as a viable small group setting is the choir. In reality, choir members are among the foremost spiritual leaders in the church—not merely because they are up front but because they lead worship. Any choir that is earnest about its ministry believes itself to be in a central role within the church. I have been fortunate to work with some outstanding ministers of music, and every one of them felt deeply about this responsibility of leading others in worship.

For this reason, if for none other, having CareRings within the choir is vital. In some cases, each group will be a section of the choir. In churches with smaller choirs, there may be only two or three groups. Whatever the size, building strong bonds and an authentic community among these worship leaders is important and exciting. When they know the personal struggles each member is going through, when they have spent time listening to and praying for each other, and when they have watched other choir members find deliverance from some trial, they will lead worship from the heart.

To accomplish having CareRings in the choir, build them from choir members not already in a group that connects to their regular Sunday school class. If there are more than a couple CareRings, connect them as a "Choir District."

Realize that doing life deeply is worth the time it takes. People do not believe they are part of a church because they are involved; they feel a part of the church

> *Doing life deeply is worth the time it takes.*

when they relate to others. The strong ties of friendship hold people together more than any other force.

HOW TO CHOOSE A SMALL GROUP TYPE

Generic or seeker? Support or special interest? Covenant or discipleship? Cell or ministry? Sunday school or kids? At this point you may be wondering how your church is ever going to be able to settle on one or more types of small groups that are right for your congregation. If so, relax. As you seek God's will for this important part of your church's ministry, he will make his plan known to you.

Here are a few steps you may want to take:

- *First, have the pastor and other teachers in the church begin teaching on the subject of community some months before beginning any groups.* Sermons and lessons can focus on topics such as unity and on biblical images of the church as "Christ's body," "living stones" and "the bride of Christ." Obviously, such lessons and messages should come from the hearts of the teachers and should not be attempts at manipulation but rather genuine attempts at communicating truth from the Lord. From that biblical foundation, lead the congregation to see that one of the best ways to develop the intended qualities of the church is through small groups.

- *Second, determine the interests and felt needs of your people by using a survey.* By giving that out in a Sunday worship service, you will accomplish a couple of things. For one thing, you will be saying that this information is important. Since you are taking the time to do it during a worship service, it truly matters and has value. Also, by giving out the survey on a Sunday morning, you will get the broadest representation from your people. You will reach some in the worship service who are not present in any other service.

- *Third, hold meetings of the church leadership to make a decision.* It is crucial that the decision come from church leaders and that they buy into it fully. They need to take time to evaluate the survey results, talk about the options and seek the Lord's will in prayer. Once they've made a decision, they can begin taking the practical steps to make small groups a reality by advertising them, training leaders and organizing the kickoff.

A SPECIAL APPEAL FOR CARERINGS

As I said earlier, there is something to be said in favor of each type of small group out there. While you may start with only one type of small group for your church, eventually you will probably want to have several different types going. There is no reason, for example, why you can't have small groups for ministry teammates *and* small groups for seekers. But as you're deciding on small group types, please consider CareRings. In fact, CareRings should possibly be the *first* kind of small group you should institute at your church.

CareRings are comparatively easy to start because of their connection to your existing adult Sunday school program and, in some cases, with other ministries as mentioned above. You start them by organizing the members of your adult Sunday school classes into small groups. Perhaps not all of your class members will feel comfortable about joining a small group. And, in time, other people may want to come to the groups before they are interested in coming to the class. But at least you're starting with an existing population of people who already know one another to some extent.

But the convenience of starting CareRings is not the only reason for them. Their *value* is also great. To my knowledge, only CareRings (which connect small groups with the Sunday school) and the Flamingo Road model (which incorporates small groups into the Sunday school classes themselves) are local church models that still embrace the ministry of teaching and respect the gifting, training and leadership of those involved in adult education. I, for one, am firmly convinced that the church dare never move away from Christian education either in form, structure or substance.

> The church dare never move away from Christian education either in form, structure or substance.

A voice that sounds the clarion call for teaching is that of Christian writer and apologist Josh McDowell. In his writings and lectures across the country, he makes the case that the idea of absolute truth is vanishing from the American scene. As the concept of truth becomes more and more subjective, the idea of absolutes is increasingly suspect by those of today's postmodern era.

Younger people especially believe such statements as "murder is wrong" to be only relatively true. Therefore, if some relative is too old and feeble to live what I consider to be a productive life, it is acceptable to take his or her life.

While that illustration is a bit extreme, it makes the point. The error is to conclude that truth is what you believe it to be, not an objective fact. Another way to state this view is that truth is found in our perception of it, not in what it actually is.

You may be thinking, *What in the world does all this have to do with small groups?* Not so much with them per se. But if the more subjective approach to truth commonly exercised in small groups is not balanced with the "Thus says the Lord ..." of preaching and biblical teaching, the church will buy into moral and spiritual relativism.

We must have *both* personal discovery and biblical application in small groups *and* the clear teaching of God's Word in educational and preaching settings. Without Sunday school or adult Bible fellowships in which teachers present the timeless truths of the Word, people will eventually conclude it is all open to personal interpretation. Therefore, it is essential that we somehow use both the community building of small groups and the clear and powerful preaching and teaching ministries. In fact, if there ever was a day in which we must not give up the proclamation of the Gospel, it is today.

I'm not saying that starting CareRings is without cost. One cost is that you'll have to develop new leaders. The gifts needed for leading small groups are not the same as the gifts needed for teaching Sunday school classes. Another cost is that small groups take up time-time that can then not be devoted to any other purpose. In order to add a small group ministry, the pastor and people must be normally willing to give up a less productive, more time-consuming ministry (more on that in chapter nine).

What I *am* saying is that CareRings are worth the cost. They bring people nearer to one another and nearer to God, while continuing to honor the educational ministry of the church. They certainly deserve serious consideration as you look at the options available in the world of small groups.

Chapter Four:
A New Reformation: The Universal Ministry of the Saints

Martin Luther was right—just not right enough! The great reformer of the sixteenth century accurately reflected biblical teaching when he declared the universal priesthood of the saints. The rending of the veil in front of the temple's Holy of Holies symbolized the truth that a way has been made for each of us to enter the presence of God (Matt. 27:51). In light of Jesus' having "gone through the heavens," the writer of Hebrews urged, "Let us then approach the throne of grace with confidence, so that we may receive mercy and find grace to help us in our time of need" (Heb. 4:14, 16). So it's true, as Luther said, that we all can approach God without using a professional priest as an intermediary. We're priests ourselves.

But another truth Luther and other reformers neglected to promote (or at least to promote enough) was the universal ministry of the saints. This truth was understood in the New Testament era. But somehow it has been lost over the years, and even the Protestant Reformation failed to restore it fully to the consciousness of the great body of believers. We know of the priests' role of representing humanity's need to God, but what about presenting God to humanity? The Reformation reaffirmed the universal priesthood of the saints, but did not really get to the "universal ministry of priests." The church has not exercised its liberty to witness as freely as it has expressed the joy of coming boldly before the throne. We are far more bold in praying than in sharing the Gospel. So it's time for a new reformation, a

> *The Reformation reaffirmed the universal priesthood of the saints, but did not really get to the "universal ministry of priests."*

recovery of the understanding that all believers are to use their spiritual gifts to build up others. It's our biblical right and responsibility.

The priests of the Old Testament were both intercessors for people and representatives of God to the people. Moses (who occupied the role of a priest) spoke to God about the nation of Israel. Even more often, though, God spoke to the nation through Moses. Exodus 18:15–16 tells us: "Moses answered him, 'Because the people come to me to seek God's will. Whenever they have a dispute, it is brought to me, and I decide between the parties and inform them of God's decrees and laws." Later, in Exodus 19:6, God refers to Israel both as a kingly nation (which implies their leadership of other nations) and as priests.

Of even more importance for us are the echoing words of the apostle Peter directed at Christians, "You are a chosen people, a royal priesthood, a holy nation, a people belonging to God, ..." (then the Greek term hina, meaning "in order that" or "so that," introduces the purpose for this separation and calling) "... that you may declare the praises of him who called you out of darkness into his wonderful light" (1 Peter 2:9). The verses that follow make it clear that the purpose for all of this is that non-Christians will see and believe the Gospel.

Acts records that the early church spontaneously passed on news of God's works to others. It says they could not help but tell the wonderful things God had done (Acts 4:20). Early church history records the words of Stephen, Polycarp and hundreds of others who could not help but share their faith even though they lost their lives for doing it. Are we as dedicated to doing the will of God in our world today? Are we unable to keep ourselves from telling about Christ, or more likely, do we have a hard time forcing ourselves to do so?

Small groups are the best available vehicle for the reformation that's needed today. In a small group, all have a chance to minister to others and to be ministered to in return. And in small groups we can develop spiritually so that we are equipped to minister in other arenas as well. Because of small groups, the Gospel can spread like never before since New Testament times.

But before we get to the contribution small groups can make in the area of ministry, let's examine Scripture's teaching on the matter more closely.

THE BIBLICAL BASIS FOR UNIVERSAL MINISTRY

We could identify many things from the biblical record that show us our universal ministry. For one, we can say that to "go into all the world and preach the good news to all creation" is our work (Mark 16:15). Like Christ, we could respond that it is "to seek and to save what was lost" (Luke 19:10). Some say it is to minister to those in need: the hungry, widows and orphans (Deut. 24:19). Others might conclude that it is to "make disciples," as Jesus told us in Matthew 28:19. Actually, all four are correct.

But the question remains, is there a "universal ministry"? Is there some common purpose we as Christians must serve? The bottom line of all this is that Jesus came in a redemptive mission. He came to reconcile all things to himself. In short, he came to change lives.

If we want to be Christlike, we will accept his purpose and mission as our ministry. This means many different things to different people. To some, it is social service—caring for the bodies and souls of people. To others, it means evangelism—restating the claims of the Gospel to win the lost. And to others, the redemptive mission of Christ is best expressed as living out their lives as silent witnesses in the world around them, being yeast in the loaf.

Regardless of the way ministry is expressed, one thing is certain: the life of a Christlike person is *not* one of a spectator. Whatever being a Christian means to you, however you would express it, you dare never live out Christianity on the sidelines. This is not a spectator sport. Christ did not call us to be observers or even casual participants. The Lord Jesus Christ wants men and women involved in serving. He is looking for people of dedication to commit themselves to him and his church in action.

A central concept of the New Testament is spiritual gifts. According to Ephesians 4, Romans 12 and 1 Corinthians 12, God has given at least one spiritual gift to every believer. He has equipped us with those gifts so that we may minister to others. Ephesians 4 summarizes it well: "It was he [God] who gave some to be apostles, some to be prophets, some to be evangelists, and some to be pastors and teachers, to prepare God's people for works of service, so that the body of Christ may be built up" (vv. 11–12).

Here's how to find out if you have caught this vision and purpose of Christ. When you are asked the question, "How many ministers are there at your church?" what do you say? Do you count them up in your head?

"Let's see. There is the pastor, music minister, youth minister, and, uh ... well, I guess that's it. We have three." No! That's how many *pastors* you have. Now, how many *ministers* do you have? "We have as many ministers as are true Christians." That is the right answer.

In the New Testament church, *everyone* ministered. No one just sat and was entertained. So, who are the ministers to be today? Everyone. We are not truly "New Testament Christians" until we are ministering to someone. That ministry may be using your gifts of helps, service or hospitality. It may be in witnessing to the change Christ has made in your life. It could be serving food in a homeless shelter. But one thing is clear: you *will* be ministering if you're a Christian.

> *We are not truly "New Testament Christians" until we are ministering to someone.*

We will all minister in different ways. We are all different. Some of us love to give to others (indicating we may have the gift of giving). For others we are never happier than when we are sharing the ideas of the Gospel (evangelism may be our gift). Still others of us love to work behind the scenes (helping or mercy may be our gifts).

Here's the great thing about this concept: whatever we do for God, if it is in Christ's name, it is ministry. And every single one of us is needed for all the functions of the body of Christ to operate. Scriptures teach that no one is better or more necessary than any other member because he or she has a certain gift. Likewise, no one is excluded because he or she does *not* have gifts. Every part is important. Every part is enabled with a spiritual gift and granted power when the Holy Spirit is given to him or her to serve and minister.

Another New Testament analogy I love is that in which Peter calls us "living stones" (1 Peter 2:5). He teaches that each of us is just that: a living stone in the building that is the church. We all rest upon Christ the cornerstone. We all rest on someone who came before us, who told us about Christ. And we all have a part. Again, we are *all* ministers to one another—someone else is counting on our witness, our service and our ministry to them.

Build your groups on this biblical foundation. Bring people together around helping, listening to and praying for others. That's ministry. Some may host. Others will facilitate the discussion. That's their ministry. But *all* of us are involved. No spectators here. Not one sideline bench warmer in the bunch. We won't let you. We all get into the game and run our play for the team.

MINISTRY IN THE CHURCH TODAY

Today, the church has become ill in many quarters and seems to have grown weary of aggressively reaching out to the lost and presenting God's message to them. Secular humanism, situation ethics and existentialism have all taken their toll on the church. It is probably true that we live more in a pagan culture than in a "Christian America." Consequently, even within the Christian community, people are slow to share their faith. We simply are not getting to those around us.

> *The church has become ill in many quarters and seems to have grown weary of aggressively reaching out to the lost.*

The most natural setting for doing so is our neighborhoods. We spend most of our time there when we're not working. We relax and enjoy our families, work in our yards, wash our cars and do a hundred other things that bring us near our neighbors. It is easy to take a pie or some fresh-baked cookies next door. It is the most convenient and least time-consuming contact we can make.

However, many of our friends in the area around our homes may never come to a church. To us the most natural place imaginable to be with our friends and to share needs, to get support and encouragement, is the church. But not to them. We must realize that, for those without faith, churches are too big, too pretentious and even scary. As hard as it may be for us to imagine, others misinterpret our churches as spiritual clubs, elitist fraternities or exclusive cults.

What can we do? We can pray faithfully that God will rekindle a vision within us to touch their lives. We can join with others who will share the burden and together try to reach others who are without God. Perhaps the most natural way we can reach others is in our homes. There we are comfortable and relaxed—as will be our friends and neighbors who visit with us there. A small group meeting in our home is a great place to get about the business of ministry.

But will we give it the time it deserves?

THE PROBLEM OF BUSYNESS

One needs to be in ministry only a few months before he or she becomes aware of a common malady. Whether we are in full-time ministry or are volunteering to lead some kind of church project, we commonly hear "I'd love to help, but I'm just too busy."

Life today is jam-packed with good and worthwhile interests. A couple with two school-aged children can be run ragged with trips to the dentist, soccer practice, music lessons, school activities, choir, band or play performances. They will also want to do their part as a citizen and volunteer time for a community service, some fund-raiser for a worthy cause or a service club.

Everything we own also owns a part of us. Our cars have to be washed, the lawn mower blade has to be sharpened, the swing set bolts have to be tightened, clothes have to be washed and the pet needs to be groomed. Then we have to get the latest computer program installed, check for e-mails, return phone calls, go to the store, pick up the cleaning, and so on, and so on.

In the midst of this hubbub it is no wonder that, when approached about small groups, people say (or at least think), "I'm just too busy." We are in love with gadgets, caught up in fads and engaged in causes. We're so enamored with time-saving devices that we have no time for spiritual development. We're overworked, underpaid, overtaxed, undernourished and overextended.

So, how do we work our way out of this predicament? We can't sell the kids, move into a tent and ride a bike to work. What can we do? For one thing, we can stop and evaluate our priorities. We can ask ourselves whether we're working harder at winning our kids to God or to ourselves. A dear friend of mine, and a man I highly admire, Don Wellman, once told me, "Dave, I have watched scores of people win their kids to themselves and lose them to God, but in 22 years of ministry, I have yet to see one couple win their kids to God and lose them to themselves." I agree.

Once we realize our priorities are out of whack, what next? How do we get off the merry-go-round? First, don't jump. I've seen a few families face this question and switch from being enveloped by materialism to utterly rejecting it. I'm not sure that's necessary, though it might be the lesser of two evils. The Bible calls for balance. There should be an equal amount of concern for spiritual well-being and for physical well-being. We ought to strive to do both: maintain a life and mature spiritually.

Exactly how any individual can achieve such a balance will depend on that person's situation. But it certainly should be a goal for everyone, so that they can be a part of a small group where they will encounter God and God's people more up close than ever.

Making Time to Join a Small Group

To those who say they are too busy for a small group, I have to say, "That's exactly the reason why you must join one." My mom used to say, "Busy hands are happy hands." But hands too busy to give God and other Christians quality time each week are simply too busy. It is that very absorption with those good possessions, activities and work that must be laid aside in the interest of spiritual and social health. There is a way out. One less trip to that practice, performance or play will not ruin our children. In fact, some groups today are finding the best thing they can do for their families is include them in their CareRing. This tells our children that the Bible is just as important as baseball practice, that learning to care is every bit as essential as learning to kick or catch, that praying matters just as much as playing.

> To those who say they are too busy for a small group ... "That's exactly the reason why you must join one."

Ask yourself honestly, *Does my schedule say God is important to me and to my children? Do the things I have committed myself to give my children the clear message that my relationship with the Lord and other Christians is worth working on?* If your answer to both questions is no, you're too busy. These tough questions may lead you to the most important answers in the life of your family.

Making Time to Lead a Small Group

Beyond the need to be in a CareRing is the importance of helping lead one. There is a great difference between attending a group and hosting or leading one. In one case we are consumers, and in the other we are contributors. On one hand, we receive; on the other, we give. It is the difference between being there to get and being there to give. It often doesn't look this way to people, but the more rewarding purpose is giving, not getting.

As part of the new reformation, the church today needs to become proactive. There is greater joy in leading than in following. You will be far more fulfilled serving than in sitting. It is a blessing to be in a group where lives are changed, but it is exhilarating to be part of bringing the change about—leading the CareRing. Can you imagine how exciting it is to help bring change in someone's life?

> *There is greater joy in leading than in following. You will be far more fulfilled serving than in sitting.*

To be effective as a small group leader, invest yourself in others. In chapter eight we'll discuss a process in which people can go through the training cycle. They will share leadership, be evaluated and then be invited to formal training. They do all this in order to become a CareRing Shepherd. This is a valuable concept to learn. Only when we reproduce ourselves in others will our ministry broaden and extend into the lives of some we'll never meet. If everyone in the new reformation has a ministry, then we become part of God's best plan when we are finding potential leaders and developing others. That is true when we let others develop us. When we are teachable, we allow someone to prepare us.

Another part of this process in the new reformation is training. That does not mean we must get a seminary education or even finish college before we can make a significant contribution. But it does mean we need to be prepared. My philosophy of leading others is summarized best by the little adage, "An ounce of prevention is worth a pound of cure." It is far easier to prevent a problem before it develops than it is to correct one after it has grown and hurt innocent people. I have learned that when we do thorough training up front we can deal with problems as they come up. When we covered the material in the beginning before a person starts to lead, we have laid a foundation upon which to build his or her leadership. I can't stress this strongly enough.

Some object, saying, "Well, that's all a waste of time. Let them get experience. After all, that's the best teacher anyway." I agree, to a point. Experience teaches far better than simply telling someone how to do it. Yet training should include experience. Class training must always be coupled with on-the-job training and actual experience. We offer both a day of initial training and a mentor to lead and develop the apprentice leader (that's what we call one who is in training to lead). We'll cover more of this later.

Offering a quality training program does not mean every church must have an expert in small groups on staff. Many of the churches where I consult bring me in for a weekend with the express purpose of providing intensive training for their leaders and potential leaders. They do this as they start or develop small group ministries. They are wise. This way they get most of the essential information up front and avoid making errors others have made. They do not have to learn from their mistakes like we have from ours. These churches can incorporate the best of what someone else has to offer, and adapt it to fit their situation. Further, the cost is very low compared to hiring a staff member.

Another effective idea is to set aside one evening a week, as my friends Jim and Karla do. Every Thursday, for more than three years now, they conduct outreach in their home. Sometimes they invite someone who is new to their church over for dinner. Often there will be business associates from Jim's company present. And normally those people will have been invited for an informal evening with one or two other couples from their church. What a simple yet powerful idea! If only half the Christians in America did this, we would dramatically reduce resistance to Christianity and open thousands of doors to the lives of others.

It is here that small groups enter the picture. When we use them with Sunday school, they are called CareRings because they are circles or "rings" of giving, caring people opening their homes to others. So much of what we want—and need—to do cannot be done in Sunday school. There simply is not enough time. But on a weeknight, the lesson of the Sunday school could be developed and applied to our lives. We could discuss ways God might want to use us and enable us to apply his Word to our lives.

> *They are called CareRings because they are circles or "rings" of giving, caring people opening their homes to others.*

So, let's get about the Father's business. Let us, with hearts broken for those who are lost, and with a new resolve to reach them, go to where they are. We don't need to haul them into our churches. Let's go to them! Let's reach out in the most convenient and natural of all surroundings—our homes—and touch hurting people.

GROUPS NEED FAT LEADERS

In the Reformation, there were leaders in all sections of Europe. It was Luther in Germany, Zwingli in Switzerland and Calvin in France. Others followed and assumed leadership after them in the Protestant Reformation. Similarly, the new reformation needs leaders. Probably not many of us are Luthers or Calvins. But that is precisely the point. The leadership we need is not one of a few but one of many! This is not a reformation of the clergy but of the laity. It is a return to the concept that all who are justified and redeemed have a vital part in ministry.

There is a very small list of qualifications for these leaders beyond their salvation. God does not always need highly skilled men and women through whom he can work. He simply needs faithful, available and teachable people!

Faithful: The first, and perhaps the most important, quality needed in a small group leader is faithfulness. First Corinthians 4:2 is clear on this subject. "Now it is required that those who have been given a trust must prove faithful." Only the "unfaithful servant" in one of Jesus' parables was dealt with severely by the Lord (Matthew 25:14-30). It is not effectiveness that seems to matter with God as much as faithfulness!

Available: For any ministry to be effective, God must work with and through people. We must make ourselves available to him. His work must be a priority for us, and that means putting other good and valuable interests and concerns aside for him and others. It means making our time, our effort and especially ourselves available. This may involve setting limits on the amount of time we'll spend on other interests—as good as they may be.

Teachable: Teachable people are a joy to work with. We're not talking about those who follow with mindless abandon the instructions of others, rubber-stamping any idea that is presented. Teachable people are those who listen for anything new or helpful, ready to incorporate that into their ministry and service. They do not have a haughty spirit or a "been there, done that" attitude. As a pastor for 22 years and a college religion department professor, I have learned that, no matter how carefully I have studied some subject for a sermon or lesson, there is always someone out there who has an insight I had missed. No matter how many times I have done something, there is always room for improvement. Be teachable, ready to learn, to grow spiritually and to develop your ministry.

Chapter Five:
Mission Accomplished: How CareRings Can Fulfill the Mission of Your Church

A few years ago, the church I pastored—Central Community Church of Wichita, Kansas—conducted a study of the mission statements of local churches across the nation. We came to a surprising conclusion. All but two or three of the statements included these five subjects: evangelism, worship, education, community building and training. They used different terms, but when you boiled it all down, these five areas formed the essence of nearly every mission statement.

Based on that information, we set out to design our own Central Community Church statement of mission. And here it is: "To change lives, transforming uncommitted people into fully devoted followers of Christ." We break this down into five purpose statements that we call "the Five E's":

- Evangelize the lost (outreach)
- Exalt God (worship)
- Educate for maturity (discipleship)
- Equip for ministry (service to others)
- Encourage God's family (fellowship)

The interesting thing for me, as the church's small group pastor, is that our CareRings contribute to the achievement of all five of these purposes. Each group includes an element of worship, usually through singing. That's *exaltation*. There is always some form of learning, since every CareRing includes Bible application. That's *education*. At the heart of our groups is caring for one another's needs. That's *encouragement*. The motivating drive for groups, however, is not meeting our own needs but meeting the spiritual needs of others. That moves us toward *evangelism.* And small groups are places where people are identified as leaders and are given training. That's *equipping* for ministry.

> *By achieving these five purposes, our CareRings are helping us accomplish our overall church mission.*

By achieving these five purposes, our CareRings are helping us accomplish our overall church mission. Through CareRings we are changing lives and transforming uncommitted people into fully devoted followers of Christ.

If your mission statement is like ours, and like those of most other churches in America, CareRings can help you accomplish it.

MISSION IN LIFE

Within the past four or five years, I have become convinced that churches commonly do everything toward reaching their mission, except communicate and work with their people to actually know and strive to live out the mission. In far too many congregations the mission statement is just a great slogan—a statement laboriously created in board meetings and then placed in a file in the office. At best, the statement appears weekly somewhere in the bulletin. Maybe it appears on a plaque on some office wall. But unless you can stop individuals leaving church on Sunday morning and ask them what the mission of the church is, and then hear at least 90 percent of them quote the mission statement correctly, it really isn't your mission. Let me say it again: If your people don't know what your mission is, then it is not your mission, regardless of how firmly the pastor or staff believes it is. Somehow it has to be worked into the thoughts and experiences of your people.

There is no better way to reach a church's objective than to involve everyone in working toward its accomplishment, and that's what CareRings do. One way to look at it is that a CareRing ministry is the church organized to fulfill its God-ordained mission. CareRings are the means to the end

> *There is no better way to reach a church's objective than to involve everyone in working toward its accomplishment, and that's what CareRings do.*

of training, motivating and involving as many people as possible in fulfilling the church's purposes.

Even when compared with the Sunday school (which has a long and established record of mobilizing church members to ministry), far more people can be involved in small groups. For example, every CareRing needs a host home, and so, with very little training, a host is involved in ministry. There are many people who love to serve in this way. To them, their home is a means of ministry, and often they do not have the up-front type of personality of those who choose to lead. Hosts are fulfilled and rewarded when they can open their home and use it for hospitality.

Another example: Through CareRings you can find many people who are leaders in the rough. They have the potential for leading but have not come to the place where they *believe* they can lead. With encouragement, they normally come to identify their ability, build confidence and sharpen their people skills. They move along quickly toward maturity when there is a solid system that can take them through training, apprenticeship and the other parts of the process. (This is one reason why being organized is important.)

The major advantage to the CareRings multiplication process is that everyone is understanding and working together toward the mission of the church. The mission statement should be quoted in training sessions, in leadership team meetings and in leadership summits every time you meet. Every setting along the way offers an excellent opportunity to remind your people of why they are there and what they believe God wants you to do as a church. This is invaluable. It makes the mission live. It focuses your efforts and gives purpose to everything you do.

In other words, small groups are not ends in themselves. They are one excellent means of reaching the lost and folding in the found. They are a method by which you can keep your people united around the purposes for which God has raised you up as a congregation.

For someone new to your church (or perhaps new to Christianity), many things can be difficult to understand. Some of your songs use words that are not familiar to people who have not attended church much of their lives. Some translations of the Bible

> *Small groups ... are a method by which you can keep your people united around the purposes for which God has raised you up as a congregation.*

have words in them that the seeker may never have heard. Even an observance as familiar to you as baptism or Communion may strike the unchurched as a mystery. The newcomers often act as though they understand it to avoid being singled out or looking uninformed. But they really don't know what these observances mean. If they knew a few people closely and trusted some friends they visited with each week, then they could easily ask and be helped to understand without fear of rejection or embarrassment.

This is another way small groups can help you fulfill the mission of your church. CareRings put people in natural settings (the home) with others they get to know and trust so that they can ask questions and lovingly be helped to see what you are doing and why you do it. This process allows people to learn and grow in the least threatening setting. It also provides the most effective setting in which newcomers are accepted and truly "belong." I saw this dramatically illustrated when I received this letter from Mary Green:

Dear Pastor,

Do you know how hard it is to find a new church in Wichita, or maybe any town?

We moved to Wichita from a small southwest Kansas town and were excited about attending Central Community. We attended services numerous times when we visited our children in Wichita. We were always blessed by the music and the messages we heard. We weren't prepared for what we experienced—both here and at a couple of other churches that we visited trying to find a church home.

We had been actively involved in a small church and part of a caring, friendly church family. We were anxious to find new Christian friends here when we had to relocate. We came to church each Sunday and were greeted at the door but that was about it. We joined a new Sunday school class that was forming and were hopeful that here was where we'd find the social times contact we were looking for. That was not the answer.

We came to Wednesday night services a few times and thought that maybe in a smaller group people would reach out to welcome us. We were wrong again. Do you know that you can be lonely surrounded by Christian people? Believe me, you can be and I was! People were hugging and laughing and enjoying each other and I was on the outside of the circle, only an observer.

We heard about CareRings so I made a phone call to the church. We were invited to attend one, which we did. The next Sunday we saw some of those people at church and exchanged greetings. We finally knew someone at church who spoke to us! A new CareRing was forming closer to our home and we were asked to join them. That enlarged our circle of friends.

Through our CareRing we finally found someone to care about us, to know when we had a death in our family and send flowers and cards, to share our prayer requests with, and most important to us, Christian fellowship.

Corporate worship is wonderful, but look around and watch for those who need someone to reach out to them, to acknowledge their presence, to ask their name.

CareRings was the answer for our need to belong! It gave us people to care for and pray for; as well as having someone care about us, someone to know our name.

In Christian Love,

Mary Green

As valuable as the Sunday school is, some people are intimidated by the learning setting. They don't want to appear dumb. They are threatened by the knowledge of the teacher and often by the knowledge of others in the class. In small groups, however, participants are learning and growing together. They intentionally state up front that none of them is the expert. They are all sitting around in a circle on the same level and sharing opinions. No one is intimidated. Thus, the newcomer has a comfortable place to speak and to listen. Over time, he or she learns what the church is all about and what it believes.

Whether newcomers or old-timers, people will live out your church's mission if they're in small groups.

CareRings—MUSCLE FOR YOUR MISSION

Many churches have discovered that they have to translate their mission into the language of the people in the congregation. In other words, they have learned that quoting the mission statement regularly, putting it in the worship folder or weekly bulletin, even posting it throughout the church building is not enough to get the mission into the hearts of the people. Many congregations have found that they must present the basic concepts of their mission before their people regularly and in a variety of ways. They have found that people do not own a concept unless it touches their hearts as well as their minds. Here small groups can help.

Like many pastors, Dr. Stan Toler works hard to cast a vision for his church. Over a four- to six-week period (usually around January), he makes the church's mission a major focus. He preaches about it. Teachers teach about it. Leaders speak about it. And all of this is effective. But in the 1990s, when I was on staff with Dr. Toler at First Church of the Nazarene in Nashville, I suggested that we could cast the vision even more effectively in small groups. So, during "vision month" each group leader led his or her group in a study of the biblical basis of the church's mission. This was said to all those in small groups, "We share the vision being cast by our leaders, so let's all pray and work to see those dreams come true."

Whether or not you want to use this kind of annual emphasis on your church's mission in your small groups, you can still find ways to disseminate the mission through your CareRings on an ongoing basis. To do this, many fellowships build the foundational concepts of their mission into small group Bible studies and applications. In this way the mission is presented to participants by the leader they know best.

Further, when leaders directly relate the mission of their small group ministry to that of their church, two things are accomplished: (1) People learn that the small group ministry is an integral and strategic part of their church, thus helping it to fulfill its purposes; (2) People see that what they do week after week in their group is all part of what their whole congregation believes its overall purpose to be.

Think of the mission statement of the local church as the skeleton. Absolutely everything that the congregation does should connect to that skeletal framework of the mission. So, for example, teaching has purpose if it educates the people toward the mission of the church. And preaching is valuable if it contributes in some way to the mission to which that fellowship has committed itself. Similarly, small groups are making a contribution to the whole structure if they are related to the mission. Therefore, much like bones are connected to muscles by ligaments, so will a common mission connect small groups to the whole mission of a church.

Every part of the human body must be healthy and operate in coordination with all other members for that body to be whole and function with power and grace. Similarly, when the purposes of the whole fellowship are lived out within each CareRing, the whole church is coordinated and is stronger. It's like putting muscle on bones. Only then is there coordination and strength. In fact, one might say that only when muscles are operative and connected to the skeleton is there life and movement.

YOUR MISSION TAKEN TO HEART

As people hear about the victories in each other's lives in groups each week, they become excited about what they believe God wants them to do and be in connection with their mission. There is nothing as effective in burning your church's purposes into the hearts of your people as small groups. Let me illustrate.

It's one thing to know and say that God wants us to lead others to Christ; it is quite another thing for people to pray for a coworker or neighbor with their CareRing week after week and finally see that person start to attend the group. Even more so, think how exciting it will be for all those people in that group to see that lost person come to worship with them. They have all had a part in praying specifically for that person, and they feel they have a part in the victory. And they do!

> *There is nothing as effective in burning your church's purposes into the hearts of your people as small groups.*

I saw this recently in connection with a CareRing I lead. A couple from the CareRing came up to me excitedly one Sunday morning in our Sunday school classroom. They were almost jumping up and down in front of me as they said, "Guess who's here? There are two people from our CareRing in class today." There was excitement in their voices, and the big smiles on their faces told me how thrilling it was for them to see two unchurched people show up in Sunday school for the first time.

I had never seen that couple excited about our mission statement purpose to "evangelize the lost" (though certainly they believed in that purpose). Yet when their friends from that small group came, it brought the evangelistic mission of our church to life for them.

The same thing could be said of other mission purposes, not just evangelism. Take exaltation, for example. How many times have you sat in church (as pastor on the platform or parishioner in the pew), only to look around you in the middle of a worship service and notice all too many folks basically just sitting through the experience? Far too many people merely observe worship, not getting involved in it emotionally or otherwise. There is at least one common reason for this: they do not have anything invested in worship. The choir, musicians and music director all get far more out of the experience than those who are only attending the service.

But when someone in a CareRing brings her guitar and that little home group sings praises to the Lord, they are all involved in what's going on. They are too close to one another not to be. Many times I've sensed God slip into a family room and bless the hearts of those people who were actively involved in praise. At Central Community Church, one of our purpose statements says that we want to "exalt the Lord." But a far higher percentage of the members of our church become involved in worship when there are 12 gathered in a home than when our congregation of many hundreds gathers in our worship center. Why? It's too easy to sit back and "observe" worship in a crowd, but it's difficult to do that in the CareRing. Everyone will know. So the purpose of exaltation is lived out when people experience worship in their homes.

Part of the dynamic in this is that we live in a dualistic society. People adapt to the situation in which they live, even many Christians. Far too many are one type of person in church Sunday morning and another type of person altogether in their homes or in their factories. Small groups are one more setting, one additional time each week, when people think about God and can be challenged to live out the Gospel to which they say "Amen" on Sunday morning.

THE CENTRAL COMMUNITY STORY

Finally, to help you get a better sense of how CareRings can work with the total mission of a church, I want to tell you the story of an actual church—mine. What Central Community Church went through in gaining a vision for small groups and learning how to further the church's mission through these small groups is similar in some crucial respects to what every church goes through.

In 1985 there were approximately 500 people attending Central Community Church. The church really was "central" at that time, being located in the heart of Wichita, Kansas. But the leaders saw the need to relocate if they were going to grow. So in that year the congregation purchased 61 acres in western Wichita and laid plans to build an educational unit and a worship center capable of seating more than 3,000. They moved into the new facility four years later.

But 1985 was a significant year for our church in another respect, for it was in that year that the pastor, Ray Cotton, caught the vision for small groups. He took several leaders to Seoul, South Korea, to see the work God was doing in Paul Yonggi Cho's Yoido Full Gospel Church, the largest church in the world. They also visited New Hope Community Church in Portland, Oregon, which offers a leading example of small group ministry. Within a year of those visits, the church leaders initiated a small group ministry at Central Community. This venture, along with a concentrated prayer ministry and the new building, caused the congregation to grow rapidly. Later, in 1996, I joined the church to help move the small groups ministry along.

Today, over 2,200 people worship at Central Community each week. The Sunday school is a vital part of congregational life, and there are between 850 and 1,000 people involved in small groups. Most of the principles discussed in this book are being used effectively at Central Community. Even during an entire year when the church was between pastors, the life and health of the congregation remained positive, largely due to the small groups.

Under the current pastor, John Henry, the groups were reorganized in 1995 to coordinate with the adult Sunday school classes. In short, each group was connected with the class to which most of its group members belonged. A district coach, called a "District Shepherd," was assigned to a huddle ("district") of three or so CareRings in that class. The church has continued to function with that organization for over five years now. In fact, three of the adult classes have more than one district. During this same period, even as new groups have been added, the adult Sunday school has continued to grow. At this writing, Central Community has the largest Sunday school among churches in its affiliation.

Central has found that one of the best ways to communicate its mission and purpose statements is through the CareRings. Often, the weekly life-change studies, called "Guidelines," are written to emphasize one or more of the mission statements. This sort of thing is not done as often nor as easily within Sunday school classes because most classes choose a curriculum from an outside publisher. Also, some of the teachers are not equipped or do not want to write their own lessons.[1]

Frequently, we urge the CareRing members to apply the truth of a given lesson in a way that will help them live out one of the purposes of our mission or the mission itself, seeking to change lives. We do this intentionally. It is part of our strategy. It is also one of the primary ways we build these values into the lives of our people.

As a result of such efforts, there are few CareRing members in our church who are not able to state the mission or purposes of Central Community Church. They know that living out these purposes is a crucial element of what it means to be a part of our community.

Another way we keep the mission of Central before our leaders is to reflect the mission and purposes of the church in the core values and purpose statements of the small group ministry. Virtually all the core values and purpose statements echo the mission and purposes of the church. (See Appendix B.)

I hope the story of Central Community Church is educational and perhaps even inspiring to you as you consider how to make small groups an integral part of your church's ministry. Through CareRings you can plant your church's mission deep in the hearts of your members and motivate them to accomplish that mission in your community for the glory of God.

Chapter Six:

A Perfect Match: Small Groups and the Sunday School

For nearly 19 years, I have led and worked with small groups. During that time, I have been exposed to virtually everything published on the subject. I've discussed small groups with more than 30 leaders of ministries in their own churches—all of those ministries having over 1,000 in attendance. And in all that time, I have never found a resource to help people understand how small groups work in churches with Sunday schools. This book is designed to meet that need.

Of course, if you recall chapter three, you remember that there are lots of different types of small groups. Many of these are not integrated with Sunday school, and yet they are serving valuable purposes. My contention is merely that there should be room in a church's ministry for small groups that are connected with the adult Sunday school program. For all that they can offer, there should be room for CareRings.

Someone may object, "I don't need to be in a group. My Sunday school class has 12 people in it, and we can all share anything we like."

My response is "I am glad you have a Sunday school class where you can share freely. Twelve is indeed a small enough number for everyone to feel comfortable opening up to each other. But are you really satisfied with the class remaining at just 12 members?"

Our eyes should be on growth, not on maintenance. We are not interested in doing just what we have been doing. We want to do it better and to bring others into the setting where it is happening.

The questions to ask yourself are: *How many new people have we brought into the class within the last year or so? And do those who have joined really feel a part of it?*

If the answer to that second question is no, it may be due to the newcomers not having a setting where they know they are accepted. Our lack of growth may be due to our unconscious resistance to adding new class members. CareRings can, in time, eliminate that resistance and allow growth to begin both within the small groups and within the Sunday school class.

> *Sunday school and CareRings have the same mission: to win, teach and disciple others .... It seems only reasonable that the two should work hand in hand.*

Sunday school and CareRings have the same mission: to win, teach and disciple others to be followers of Christ. It seems only reasonable that the two should work hand in hand. Their uniqueness qualifies them to complement one another, each providing a dimension the other does not have. Yet their similarities enable each to extend the ministry and mission of the other.

Our friends Jim and Karla provide an example of this synergistic type of "teaming" between groups and the Sunday school. Many times the couples they have invited into their home on Thursday nights have been visitors to their Sunday school class. The first time I was with them, there was another new couple and two or three regulars from the class present. It was a wonderful time to get acquainted.

And here's the best part—being new in a big church it meant a lot to me to be invited into someone's home right off the bat. I was impressed! The next week, when my wife was back in town, we both attended church there and made that our church home. We always felt welcomed because of that evening with Jim and Karla.

As we're about to see, there's much to be gained by integrating small groups with Sunday school the CareRings way.

LIMITATIONS OF SUNDAY SCHOOL

As effective as Sunday school has been for over 200 years, it has its limitations, both large and small. An example of a minor limitation of Sunday school is that many nonchurchgoers have the perception that, if they attend church and Sunday school, they have to get dressed up.

They feel they don't have the right clothes, or they just prefer to be comfortable in casual clothes. They haven't attended church in so long they don't realize that many church people have become far more casual and dress more informally than even five to ten years ago. And because of this misunderstanding, they don't give Sunday school a try.

They would not have the same misunderstanding about a small group meeting in a Sunday school class member's home on a weeknight. They would assume that everyone would dress casually, and so dress would not be a barrier for them in that setting.

As I said, that's just one example of a minor limitation of Sunday school. You could think of more, if you tried. But now I want to focus on three major limitations: the limited amount of time the class provides for Bible study, the limited opportunity Sunday school has to attract newcomers to attend and the limited amount of time a single Sunday school teacher has to follow up on absentees. In each case, small groups provide the possibility to compensate for these limitations.

The Limitation of Time

The time available for a Sunday school lesson usually ranges from 25 to 45 minutes. There is normally a gentle pressure to conclude applied by the upcoming worship service, which immediately follows the class. In many churches the choir members (and even some with other duties) have to leave five to ten minutes early. Added to this is the fact that there are always some who come late and disrupt the early part of the class. It's amazing we get anything done!

CareRings provide a setting in which we apply what has been taught in the Sunday school class. They become the life laboratory in which we test and prove the concepts and lessons of the Sunday school. Although a CareRing may never meet for more than an hour and a half per week, that is still twice the length of time devoted to the lesson in the Sunday school class. There is so much negative influence and pressure on us from the outside world that we, as Christians, need to spend more than 45 minutes a week studying the Bible and praying together. Out of 112 waking hours every week, a total of about three

> *CareRings provide a setting in which we apply what has been taught in the Sunday school class.*

hours devoted to understanding and applying God's Word doesn't seem like too much to ask.

The Limitation of Newcomer Contact

In chapter one, we discussed Leith Anderson's view that new people are now coming into the church primarily through the weekday groups and ministries. And given the choice between Sunday school and worship, people attend worship first. If he is right, there is a logistics barrier to getting people into a smaller setting than worship. Sunday school is normally over *before* the worship service, and it will not be held again for another week. It's questionable whether you'll ever get newcomers into a Sunday school class and, if they go for long without close contact with church members, they may soon drift away from the church altogether.

Wouldn't it be a great idea to have a number of group leaders available to meet visitors as they leave church and invite them to their homes for a CareRing session that very week! The setting of a home is natural. It is informal. It meets a felt need for getting to know people as people, not only as fellow worshippers. This approach would bridge the gap between the large worship setting and the personal home setting. It would also encourage the newcomers to try out the Sunday school since they now know some people who attend it.

The Limitation of Visitation

My wife and I once attended a Sunday school class of about 30 to 35 in average attendance, made up mostly of middle-aged adults (except, of course, for my wife and I, who are much younger!). It was taught by a high school coach who did an excellent job of keeping most of us involved. We all sat in a circle to urge us to participate. We enjoyed the discussion, which was mixed with a brief scriptural study. There was good rapport among the members.

With 30 or so in attendance, and with more than 50 on the roll, this class was typical of larger classes in one respect—it was not realistic to expect the teacher to call or write the 20 or more absentees. He's just one man, and he's got a demanding job and a family to keep him busy during the week. Some classes have tried to get around this problem by having members of the class do the calling or visitation. Far too often, however, contact is not made with absentees.

At one church, a survey revealed that 49 percent of the people who were missing one or two weeks did not have any form of contact by the church.[1] I was appalled and disturbed. In this busy day, with dozens of demands clamoring for people's attention, the church must reach out to people with love and concern.

If we don't follow up on our people who are missing, we are worse than the retailer who doesn't follow up on prospects or serve his or her customers. If a shop doesn't do that, it misses a few bucks. When the church doesn't follow up, we miss an eternal soul! Amazingly, we then wring our hands and shake our heads, lamenting over those who were once a part of the fellowship and "fell by the wayside." Let's be about the Father's business—caring for people!

> *If we don't follow up on our people who are missing, we are worse than the retailer who doesn't follow up on prospects or serve his or her customers.*

ADVANTAGES OF MATCHING SMALL GROUPS WITH SUNDAY SCHOOL

Some churches have recognized the limitations of Sunday school and are asking whether they ought to scrap the whole thing. I say no! Let's not do away with Sunday school. In a day of widespread ignorance about the Bible and all-too-common failure to live by biblical principles, we need the educational ministry of the church more than ever.

At the same time, of course, we have to be realistic about what Sunday school can and cannot accomplish. Where Sunday school has limitations, let's try to overcome them. One great way to do that is by augmenting Sunday school with CareRings.

Furthermore, by having both ministries in place, we can experience growth in both areas. When a visitor shows up for our Sunday school class, it's easy and natural to invite that person to come to a CareRing session during the week. It works the other way, too. A CareRing is a great event to invite unchurched friends and neighbors to. Once they attend the CareRing for a while and see that Christians are not so strange after all, they will be open to attending Sunday school and worship.

The last CareRing I started had six or eight new people attending. Of those, three of them came to Sunday school for the first time and one couple attended a class cookout.

Matching small groups with Sunday school can also help produce growth in the small group ministry. One of the feelings that militates against birthing new groups is the fear of losing friends. As groups meet, members bond with one another. They learn to love and rely on one another. Consequently, these members resist starting new groups. However, when both the original CareRing and the new CareRing are part of the same adult Sunday school class, the participants do not feel this loss as strongly. They know they will continue seeing each other every week in class. Small groups divide more easily, and the growth goes on.

Let's explore some other practical advantages of matching small groups with Sunday school.

Sharing the Caregiving and Visitation Load

In many churches, 20 percent of the laypeople do 80 percent of the work. If we really believe in the universal ministry of the saints (remember chapter four?), this is unacceptable. Ministry consultant Stan Toler suggests that pastors—and in larger churches, other staff members—should spend 80 percent of their time with 20 percent of the laypeople, training them to find, enlist and develop the other workers needed.[2] In this way, they would equip new leaders to enlarge the 20 percent involved to 80 percent or more![3]

In the meantime, we have too few people doing the caring and too many waiting to be cared for. Sunday school, on its own, can't change that. In the typical church there are maybe 10 to 20 teachers. Most of them do an outstanding job of teaching the class. Yet in many churches the teacher's position does not include responsibility for contacting absentees from their classes, much less contacting visitors who showed up only for a worship service or some other church activity.

> *We have too few people doing the caring and too many waiting to be cared for.*

While many of our churches have about half the number enrolled (on our responsibility lists) in class attendance on a given Sunday, we often have *no one at all* responsible for contacting absentees. And at least in larger classes, it is unreasonable to expect the teacher to carry this load. If a class has 20 to 30 or more on a given week, there is no way the teacher can care for them all. And even with the assistance of some class members, it is doubtful whether they can provide all the care that is needed for all the people who are involved.

But now imagine such a class that has CareRings under way. Like a class I mentioned earlier, this class has 50 on its rolls and 30 in regular attendance. How easy it would be for this class to have five groups of ten persons each. Trained group leaders could then look for only three or four of their CareRing who were missing in a given week and could follow up on them immediately. With ten in the groups, there would be room for growth. Also, on an average week, each CareRing would have about eight at the home meeting—even allowing for absentees. If CareRings were in place, it is natural for group leaders to welcome any visitors who do come to the Sunday school class and invite them to their CareRing.

As this is being written, we are seeing this very idea work powerfully in our church, Wichita's Central Community Church. Three months ago we realized we were not reaching the young married couples. We lined up couples to help lead the class, found two great teachers to share leading and teaching and started with 76 men and women our first week of the class. All but eight of these couples were new to Sunday school.

We also found seven couples who wanted to help get new CareRings started for their class. They attended training, I took them through a turbo group (more on this later) and today, within three months, we have 11 young adult couples in leadership roles as leaders, apprentices and hosts. There are four CareRings meeting each week, and the leaders are inviting others from the class to their new CareRings every week.

Here is the powerful part of this strategy: When we start new CareRings in a class, we involve those who are attending regularly, but we take it a step further. We also invite those who are on the fringes, who attend only sporadically, and who have not been folded into the life of the class. When this happens, they then become more faithful, more committed and more regular in their attendance. In this way, the CareRing Shepherd-Leaders share the caregiving and visitation load for the class. I wish you could be in this class or their CareRings to hear the exciting stories of these young men and women renewing their commitments to God, building new relationships and getting established as the people of God!

Putting the Lessons into Practice

With so little time available to the Sunday school, it is nevertheless unlikely that people would be open to expanding the time classes meet to two hours or more. Sunday morning is just too full of activity. Yet we all agree that there is a need for delving into Scripture more deeply. It makes sense, then, that we would provide a setting in our homes in which to apply what we hear taught in the class.

Picture an adult Sunday school class studying evangelism. The teacher does his or her best to cover a few key Bible passages and convey some helpful principles of evangelism to the students. But in the time available, there is little opportunity to explore any of those issues in depth or talk about applying them to actual situations in the lives of class members.

But now imagine that those same class members meet in half a dozen CareRings during the week. Each group returns to the subject of evangelism and explores it in more depth and practicality. One group member has the opportunity to get clarification on a biblical point he didn't understand during class time. Another group member asks advice from other group members about sharing the Gospel with a friend at her place of work. Each group spends time in prayer for their unsaved acquaintances. Several individuals ask for help or accountability in evangelism they are planning to do within the coming week.

Now what has become of the lesson on evangelism?

Living Out Our Responsibilities for Others

Many lessons in Sunday school deal with our practical responsibilities for others. At least 20 times now I have walked through the story of the Good Samaritan in a Sunday school class. But when does someone show me how to be a "Good Samaritan"? Where can I actually demonstrate love across racial lines and religious barriers? It's as part of a CareRing, not as part of a Sunday school class, that I can live out the example of the Good Samaritan.

Helping a coworker who has suffered the loss of a loved one, assisting a couple new to the area as they move in, taking a pie to the home of a neighbor with a new baby—these are all acts of love and compassion. Those acts speak louder than our words, and our fellow CareRing members can help us with them.

Small groups sometimes take on a special service project, having been energized by the discoveries and spiritual growth of the CareRing. They want to apply this newfound concern. They are moved with compassion and need a way to express it.

Four years ago, a terrible storm system blanketed south-central Kansas and poured down almost a foot of rain in some areas. Not far from our church a small stream overflowed and flooded scores of homes. One of these homes belonged to a couple who hosted a CareRing, Vernon and Rowena Nicholson.

Seeing the waters rise, Vernon got on the phone to a couple of CareRing members and asked for help clearing the furniture out of his basement. Within minutes, nearly two dozen people showed up to remove the piano, pool table and other furniture and valuables. A mere 20 minutes after the last of the furniture was carried up the steps to safety, the two sliding glass doors broke, flooding the basement with four and a half feet of water.

Here, before our very eyes, many of the lessons we have studied over the years in Sunday school were being lived out. The Good Samaritan had nothing on those CareRing members who spontaneously responded to a cry for help. Going the second mile, which we often teach about, was lived out that night.

It is so important to build into church life a setting in which to express the gift of shepherding. We often fail to make a direct connection between the spiritual gifts and the settings we offer in which those gifts can be exercised. Imagine what the church would be like with no preaching, evangelizing, teaching or stewardship. We have settings in which all those gifts are expressed. Yet, there is a host of gifts we do not recognize by our organization, or lack thereof. One example is shepherding. This is a leadership and pastor-type gift. We might all agree that this is a gift, and yet offer no setting in which one who has this gift of leadership and caregiving can express it.

The opposite is true of the small groups movement. Small group leaders acknowledge that teaching is a gift. And they agree that leadership of a small group is NOT primarily one of teaching. Yet some churches organize

> *When we connect small groups with the Sunday school we are making it clear that we recognize and embrace both the teaching and leading/ shepherding ministries.*

small groups separate from any teaching setting, and even encourage that they take the place of Sunday school. Granted, there are teaching opportunities other than the Sunday school, but none that more purely showcases the gift of teaching.

When we connect small groups with Sunday school we are making it clear that we recognize and embrace BOTH the teaching and leading/shepherding ministries. We make the statement: Teaching the Word (and the teaching gift) is every bit as important as fellowship and community development (and the shepherding gift).

If our only way of approaching the Bible is uniquely opinion-based, we are preparing the way for a humanist gospel. This is so important because of what we have discussed elsewhere: Namely, that today many people are coming to believe that truth is relative. We chuckle at the statement, "It doesn't matter what you believe, as long as you're sincere." Yet, we in the small group movement are on the verge of fostering that very concept within our own people. When the primary or singular setting of Bible study is subjective, then truth, as an absolute, is dealt a heavy blow. The meaning of the Word is not exclusively one of personal interpretation. There is a "thus saith the Lord" element in the true biblical message as well.

> *If our only way of approaching the Bible is uniquely opinion-based, we are preparing the way for a humanist gospel.*

True, the application of the Word is always up to us as a community in the light of our cultural context, and it is up to us personally as we live it out in daily experience. Yet, what was wrong, or right, for Moses in the Ten Commandments, for Joseph as his 11 brothers stood before him in Egypt and for David facing temptation with Bathsheba, is still wrong or right today. Moral truth is absolute.

It is not determined by the whims of our views and opinions. Truth is truth. Teaching honors that concept in a way that "sharing" does not. Preaching lifts up the authority of almighty God with certainty that discussion never will.

For this reason, we link the teaching ministry of Sunday school with the discovery methods of small groups. There is a place for both. Neither is complete without the other. They are BOTH needed, and we bless them both when we connect them with each other in the CareRings approach to small groups.

Helping Each Other Apply What the Word Teaches

I have often heard people comment during a Sunday school class discussion, "Boy, I need to work on that in my life!" or "That puts it right where I live. I really must grow in that area." A new light of understanding or conviction has dawned in the lives of those who say such things. Yet will the light grow, or will it fade out? Too often the class members move right along in their discussion, without taking the time to encourage the one who has expressed a new insight.

How great it would be if on the next Tuesday night at CareRing someone who made such a comment would now have a chance to bring the subject up again and ask for help! How marvelous it would be if a supportive and loving group of friends would gather around him or her and pray with the person for the courage to change!

Exercising the Spiritual Muscle of Prayer

As Christians, we all pray. Almost all Christians I know pray before every meal to return thanks. Most Christian parents pray every night with their children at bedtime. We all agree with the pastor during the prayers in worship (at least as long as our attention lasts) and with whoever prays for the requests mentioned in our class. Yet for many of us, those occasions just about equal the total of our prayer. The average Christian prays only about seven minutes a day.

Given our prayerlessness, it's no wonder that many, if not most, of us have never led another person to Christ. No wonder many of our prayers, when we *do* make them, seem to go unheeded. We are praying superficial prayers that amount to little more than "vain repetitions" (Matt. 6:7, KJV). We've got to do something about this! Prayer is a high and lofty business, and yet we go about it weakly.

CareRings build a section of quality prayer time into our lives at least once a week. Often CareRing members will pair up for prayer on a particular topic every day of the week. One exciting CareRing I know of will pair up for the week to pray in couples for those who are mentioned in the group as needing Christ. They agree to call one another each day and pray for that person by name. What a marvelous way to exercise the muscle of prayer!

Week after week, members of the CareRing pray together. They at least hear others bringing their needs to God. Also, one of the reasons we strongly urge CareRings to meet every week is so they can more easily share their answers to prayer and one another's victories. These activities do unbelievable things for a group, a Sunday school class, even an entire church. Can you imagine sitting down in a class where four or five groups of people prayed for each other (there is healing in that alone) and begin telling the class what marvelous things God is doing? It is wonderful!

Allowing Classes to Grow Larger

Sometimes people get the feeling they are doing well when their Sunday school class reaches about 20 or so in attendance. Often they don't even think of bringing friends or neighbors. They are content with things the way they are and don't worry much about getting others involved.

In other classes, where a passion for growth has not yet died out, they reach a certain level and don't seem to be able to break through some invisible barrier and get to a larger size. They may try any number of techniques for attracting and keeping new class members, but the class remains stuck at about where it has been for a while.

> *CareRings provide a sense of closeness that people deeply desire, even in large classes.*

What is the solution to this lack of concern for growth or for this inability to grow beyond a plateau? CareRings.

CareRings provide the opportunity and impetus for growth. They provide a sense of closeness that people deeply desire, even in large classes. And so growth naturally goes on.

Preparing Future Sunday School Teachers

Any Sunday school superintendent can tell you how difficult it is to find willing teachers. Small groups can become a proving ground where people try out their wings of leadership and build courage to later try teaching.

I have seen this process repeated three times just this year alone. I have watched three Shepherds, thinking they would never teach, start leading a group. Then, as their confidence built and as they become more experienced, they began thinking about teaching. All three of these Shepherds are presently moving into teaching slots. Two of the three have started brand new classes!

I have watched others in the class my wife and I teach first get some experience as a host of a CareRing, then lead a group and finally join the leadership and ministry team of our class. This is exciting! It is so fulfilling to see leaders emerge and confidently take their place in guiding and serving a class.

Building Visitor Follow-Up Into Our Lives

All too often visitors come to Sunday school classes and church, only to walk out the door never to be seen again. Some of this is to be expected. We can't win or keep them all. Yet I am convinced a part of the reason we lose people is that we aren't organized to follow up with them. As was mentioned earlier, how exciting it would be to have at least one group in each class to which you could invite the newcomer!

One thing that CareRings urges us to do is be on the watch for new friends. CareRings are built for, and are dependent upon, new people becoming a part of them. Note that having CareRings will not make us caring people. We will have to work at it. But they offer a setting each week in which we are reminded and encouraged to pray for and bring friends to the group.

Providing a Natural Bridge to the Church

Linking groups and Sunday school classes provides a natural bridge that new group members can easily cross to connect with the church. I saw this illustrated just this year in one of our groups.

Donna Roth, the neighbor of one of our CareRing members, Stan and Dale Weir, had lost her husband three years ago in a tragic airplane crash. She is a wonderful woman who was open and needed love. When Stan and Dale invited her to the CareRing, Donna accepted and soon found a place of love, acceptance and belonging. Just this week Donna said, "I had visited the church a couple times, but after joining the

CareRing, I knew people and felt I *belonged*. I would never have attended Sunday school if I had not *first* gotten to know people in the CareRing!" It was not long until she was invited to our Sunday school class. She quickly became involved, has grown spiritually and is today one of the *teachers* in that class!

If we are serious about making outreach one of the purposes of our groups, then it only strengthens the whole ministry to connect them to an adult education class. People most typically come to the Lord through a personal invitation. There is no better way to provide a natural way for people to connect with other Christians than through a friend in a group who is also in a Sunday school class.

> *There is no better way to provide a natural way for people to connect with other Christians than through a friend in a group who is also in a Sunday school class.*

Linking small groups and Sunday school classes gives a natural structure for district formation. As small groups develop, and the ministry grows in a local church, there must be some form of organization. This is necessary to keep leaders fresh, to help everyone stay focused and to continually keep the vision before the people. Another more obvious reason is to organize so that all leaders are resourced, encouraged, coached and loved with excellence. This reflects the ratios discussed in chapter six.

When CareRings are linked with classes, the most natural way of organizing them is to group all those in the same class together to form what we call a District Huddle. Typically, a Leader called the District Coach will come up through the ranks from among your most effective Shepherds. These people can be even more proficient when districts are arranged according to classes, because everyone already knows them. They have won the respect of leaders and class members alike. Therefore, they become even more productive.

One of the toughest things to do is get new groups birthed. Members have gotten to know and love each other. They don't want to be "taken apart" or separated from one another. Another major advantage of organizing districts by classes is that, when new groups are birthed, those members will still see each other every week. This takes much of the resistance out of rebirthing.

Linking the Sunday school and CareRings provides groups a great pool from which to draw new members and in which to start new groups. One of the most difficult things for long-time members of churches to do is to reach out to others, even Christians, who are new to them. I have seen more than a few new groups struggle getting started, straining to get group members to invite others to their group—even people in their own church.

While I sometimes don't understand why, I do know this task becomes far easier when the new group is being formed from within a Sunday school class where people are commonly visiting before and after class and where they have already built some relationships through class events, social outings, etc. If we are serious about making outreach one of the purposes of our groups, then it strengthens the whole ministry to connect them to an adult education class.

Reaching People Who Are Unavailable on Sunday

There are some people—a limited number—who would like to be in church and Sunday school on Sunday but for one reason or another cannot come. These include people in the serving professions: firefighters, police, nurses, paramedics and so on. Then there are increasing numbers these days who work in retail and are required to miss church to work in gas stations, convenience stores, restaurants, pharmacies and other places of business. Consumer convenience is the word of the day, and more businesses are accommodating those who want to purchase on Sundays. What is the church to do for people who can't show up on Sunday?

We will continually need to discover creative ways to reach these people. Another way of seeing it is that we must be more flexible to meet the changing needs of the society in which we live. That is no problem for God. The New Testament churches had no buildings, no vans or buses, no full-time paid ministers, no property—and they did quite well.

> *CareRings makes the church available to anyone on any work schedule.*

CareRings makes the church available to anyone on any work schedule. We can meet early in the morning, in the evening, in the middle of the afternoon—you name it. CareRings can accommodate those who can't make it to a class on Sunday morning.

Valuing Both Teaching and Community Building

Some congregations have abandoned the Sunday school. In my opinion, that is a big mistake. Doing so deprives people of in-depth Bible knowledge. In time Christians may become shallow. They may develop faith lacking content.

Other churches have never bothered to begin a small group ministry. That's an equally big mistake. Such churches miss the value of establishing accountability and developing intense personal community. They may have knowledgeable members, but those members are not as connected as they could be and ought to be.

But when both Sunday school and small groups are available, someone who participates in both ministries gets well-rounded support from his or her church. That person is then equipped to become the kind of Christian who can make a powerful impact on this needy world of ours.

TIME OUT FOR A PROGRESS CHECK

Before we go any further, let's take a look back at where we've been. In chapter one we learned that small groups are based on biblical principles, meet key human needs and form one of the three major spheres of church ministry. In chapter two we took a tally of some of the major benefits a small group ministry can confer on a church. In chapter three we stepped back and took a panoramic view of the different models and types of small groups. In chapter four we opened our eyes to the biblical vision of the universal ministry of the saints—a vision that small groups can help make a reality through a "new reformation." And in this chapter we have made a case for combining Sunday school with those special small groups called CareRings.

If at this point you're not convinced of the value of small groups in general and CareRings in particular, well, there is probably nothing more I can say to persuade you. You might as well put this book down. But if (as I suspect) you are by now thoroughly primed with the idea that CareRings can be of great value to the church you are a part of and love and want to help, then you're going to find the coming chapters to be tremendously useful.

We're about to turn to the practicalities of implementing a CareRings ministry in your church. Get ready for tested advice about organizing, kicking off and leading CareRing groups. Open your mind to creative thinking about how you and others in your church can adapt the information and put into place a CareRings ministry for your fellowship.

The adventure in caring is really getting going now!

Chapter Seven:
Let's Get Organized! The Basics of Putting Together a CareRing Ministry

Recently the Lord laid it on my heart to start a CareRing for people with spouses who are not Christians. We announced the idea, collected names of potential members and found a host home. The group began meeting. Most of those who have been coming are women, and I noticed that they began bonding with one another within a couple of months. They talk with one another on the phone during the week, praying with each other for the salvation of their husbands. It was a wonderful surprise when I first observed this bonding happening. Yet a couple of greater surprises were still to come.

First, one of the members of the CareRing—a woman who had previously never been a part of our Sunday school class—suddenly began showing up at class time. The class was mentioned only a couple times in the CareRing, but there she was. Later, one of the wives in the CareRing brought her husband to a cookout sponsored by the Sunday school class. She had attended the class before, but her husband had never shown up for any church event. These were breakthroughs for both couples.

How did such happy events come about? Did we apply pressure to the CareRing members to get themselves and their spouses involved in Sunday school? No. We didn't even make calls to invite these two women to the activities. It was just the natural thing for them to do, since they knew me, knew each other and wanted to grow spiritually. Now we have a broader setting to which we can invite their spouses.

And as our CareRing continues to meet, we trust the Lord that the spouses *will* come to the church—and to the Lord himself—someday.

That kind of spiritual impact is what CareRings are all about. But what enabled it to happen? What sort of organization was there behind the scenes that the members of my CareRing could only have glimpsed?

This chapter will reveal how a CareRing ministry is structured to enable the work to get done without anyone being overburdened.

CareRing Organization: Fitting It All Together

As we begin looking at the organization of a CareRing ministry, it's important to note a couple of things. First, organization is never an end in itself. The CareRing structure is not the purpose for the ministry; it is only the setting within which we get people connected, won to the Lord and built up in the most effective ways. Second, the organization you will find described in this chapter is adaptable. For example, if you have a very small adult Sunday school program, you may begin with only one or two CareRings and therefore won't need to put in place a full-scale huddle organization (until you grow!). The organizational principles presented here are time-tested, but ultimately you'll have to put together a CareRing ministry that works for *your* church.

With those clarifications in mind, we can begin taking a look at the pieces that make up a typical CareRing ministry. In a nutshell, here's how it goes: One or more CareRings are formed with members of an adult Sunday school class. From two to five CareRings are linked together in something called a "district huddle." Each CareRing has its facilitator, called a "shepherd-leader," or just a "shepherd." A leader-in-training is called an "apprentice leader."

The district huddle is headed up by someone called a "district coach," who may be training an "apprentice coach"—that's someone getting ready to lead a group of CareRings in a district huddle of his own. If there are two or more district coaches within a Sunday school class, then they are managed by a "district coaches' coordinator." The whole ministry is overseen by the "small group pastor." Here's how it might look:

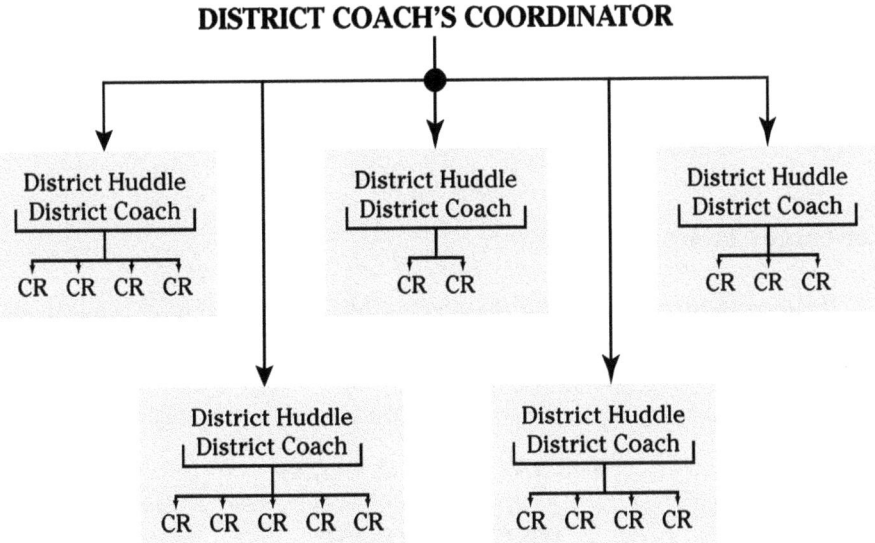

Classes, Groups and District Huddles

As you've already learned, CareRings are designed to work with an existing adult education program in a church. At least initially, CareRings are made up of members of a Sunday school class. As the CareRing starts, members of a CareRing invite others to join the small group. These people may or may not be in a Sunday school class, though it is hoped that they eventually will be. Likewise, newcomers to a Sunday school class will be invited to join one of the CareRings associated with the class. So normally there remains a strong overlap of membership between a CareRing and the adult Sunday school class with which it is associated. And meanwhile, both the educational ministry and the small group ministry are growing.

Let's say you have a popular Sunday school class made up of about 20 married couples who have children. If most of the class members are interested in being a part of a CareRing, you could start as many as four CareRings with about eight or ten members apiece. You may have

CareRings within other Sunday school classes in your church as well, but the CareRings associated with the married-couples-with-kids class would be linked together as a "district huddle." There would be one leader (the district coach) overseeing all the groups in this district huddle.

A large church might have many district huddles. For example, they might have four or five adult Sunday school classes, each with anywhere from one to six CareRings. These CareRings would be linked in district huddles in the most convenient way possible, but never with more than five CareRings per district huddle.

For Large Classes

If there is more than one district huddle in a Sunday school class, a "district coaches coordinator" serves to work in the class. Then the organizational structure looks like this:

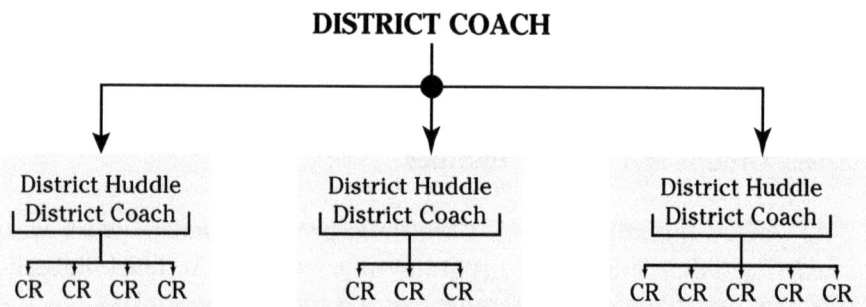

One of the main advantages of a district organization is that this approach maximizes the abilities of lay leaders. They are given places of leadership and are released to serve. In this environment where trust is fostered, many leaders flourish. My belief is that when people are trained, coached and released to ministry, they rise to the opportunity. I have seen leaders build strong teams of enthusiastic leaders, who in turn provide visionary leadership for those in their care.

One question that often comes up is, "If CareRings are connected with Sunday school classes, what happens when you have so many

CareRings in a class that you can start new district huddles associated with that class?" There are at least two possibilities:

- **Start a new Sunday school class.** This, in fact, is one of the great advantages of connecting small groups and Sunday school. It is easy to form new classes with people who already know each other deeply. Of course, for this approach to work, you'll need a new teacher, an additional room for the new class, and so on.

- **Have two or more district huddles within the class.** In this way there is an option to those new to the class. They can choose to join a group connected with either district huddle.

I am seeing this being effectively done now where I serve. One of our classes, "The High Adventure Class," has grown rapidly to over 150 attenders. Their district huddle now has six CareRings. Part of the way they have grown is that about 40 singles have become a part of the class. Singles leadership is soon to be in place, allowing the class to have a huddle for couples and another for singles. There could be no more excellent way to minister to singles than to help them know they are part of the class, and yet enable them to build strong bonds with other singles in CareRings.

CareRing Shepherd-Leaders

The burden of leadership is shared in a CareRing ministry. Those with the appropriate gifts are tapped for their service, but no one is given so much responsibility that it becomes unbearable.

Some persons who have a kind of leadership role are the hosts. These are the couple (of course, it could be a single person, too) who open their home for a CareRing every week. Apart from offering comfortable living space for up to 12 persons to meet in at the same time each week, the hosts serve by making their guests feel welcome and by providing name tags. The spiritual gift that comes into play for them is hospitality.

But of the four primary leadership roles in a CareRing ministry, shepherding is the gift that is most valuable. Other gifts I have seen used very effectively are leadership, faith, encouragement and discernment. (See Appendices C, D and E for more information about these roles.)

The group leader. Each CareRing has a Shepherd-Leader who coordinates the sessions. This person is not a teacher. He or she is not primarily conveying information. Rather, this person is primarily seeing that the group members are properly taken care of. The Shepherd-Leader makes sure things get done and people are having their spiritual needs met.

A CareRing session has three primary aspects: Bible study, prayer and worship. The CareRing Shepherd-Leader may not lead in all three parts of the session, but he or she makes sure that someone does. Ultimately, he or she is responsible for seeing that things get done. As others lead and help, the Shepherd is always observing them, looking for future leaders. The Shepherd-Leader also coaches potential leaders.

The Shepherd-Leader is like a sergeant on the front lines, like a supervisor of the employees who make the product. He or she is right where the action is. It's an exciting role and one that can have an eternal impact on the souls of people who show up for the CareRing. This is shepherding at its purest.

The district coach. When two or more CareRings have been started, it's best to group them together in a district huddle. And the one who heads up the district huddle is the district coach. This person is usually a former group leader who amassed some useful experience in CareRings and proved himself or herself especially gifted in this kind of ministry. Now, as a district coach, this person has gone on to provide support to the group leaders under his or her control, especially in the area of encouraging growth and the birth of new groups.

As a part of your initial and ongoing training, you'll want to stress the importance of building a strong team. Leadership is a vital role for the district coach. You'll want to emphasize how important it is to live a vital life of devotion to God. Spiritual piety is essential. You'll also urge the district coach to challenge and inspire his or her leaders, apprentices and hosts. Therefore, motivational skills are valuable. So, leadership, spirituality and motivational skills are the three big roles the district coach must play. It is also essential that the district coach loves people, is dedicated to the

> *Leadership, spirituality and motivational skills are the three big roles the district coach must play.*

success of his or her leaders, and that he or she strives to continue growing as leaders and servants of the Lord.

The primary setting of ministry for the district coach is within the district huddle. They focus on the spiritual health and maturity of their leaders. They constantly keep the tasks of raising up other leaders before their group leaders.

The district coaches' coordinator. In a class containing two or more district huddles, there may be a need for someone to be a district coach to the coaches. This person is the district coaches' coordinator.

Most churches won't need a district coaches' coordinator. But in large churches with large Sunday school classes and lots of CareRings, it can be helpful to have a person in this position. At our church we have a district coaches' coordinator in one class, and as we continue to grow we'll presumably need more of them.

The ideal district coaches' coordinator is someone who has been a group leader and a district coach and has shown exemplary dedication and ability in these roles. He or she can move on to provide support and counsel for the district coaches.

The small group pastor. Overseeing the entire CareRing ministry is the small group pastor. Usually this is a paid, professional member of the church's pastoral staff. If a small church has only one pastor, then that person takes on this role. Often a lay leader can serve well as a director of your CareRing ministry. If so, be sure this role is *all* they are asked to do within the church. In a larger church, an associate pastor or other staff member may have this responsibility. Ideally, the small group pastor is someone who is entirely dedicated to growing small groups in the church, including CareRings. Regardless, this individual is the one who sets the tone for the whole ministry. This person should be someone who is strongly gifted for ministry and has a deep passion for small groups.

The small group pastor is a shepherd of shepherds. He or she appoints district coaches and then works with them to develop their skills at growing the CareRings under their care. He or she makes sure the leaders within the ministry have the necessary training and trouble-shoots problems as they arise. But this person should never let maintenance of the ministry obscure the objective of growing the

CareRings ministry and, with it, the adult Sunday school program of the church.

SPANS OF CARE: KEEPING THE GROWTH GOING

One of the most common errors committed in small group ministries is expecting ministry leaders to handle more than they are capable of. What happens when a manager in a company has 25 people reporting directly to him? What happens when nursery volunteers fail to show up at your church and one unlucky teenager is left with 18 screaming infants in his or her charge? Things get out of control quickly. People who ought to have been cared for are overlooked. The same things can happen in a small group ministry unless you take care to break down the responsibilities appropriately at every level.

That's why it's important to pay attention to what is called the "span of care." This is the number of people each leader in the ministry is directly responsible for. It's normally expressed in terms of a ratio. A span of care of 1:5, for example, means that one person is responsible for five other persons. The larger the number of persons one is responsible for, the greater the span of care. Too great a span of care for a leader can mean trouble. Always keep in mind the span of care.

For a CareRings ministry, there are three spans of care you must know about. The maximum span of care for a group leader is 1:12. The maximum span of care for a district coach is 1:5. And the maximum span of care for the pastor who is coordinating the CareRings ministry is 1:10. The differences among the ratios is due to the nature of the leaders' work.

Let's take a look at each span of care.

The Group Leader's Span of Care

When a CareRing grows to about a dozen people, it's time to start thinking about birthing a new group. This is not because the leader loses control when the group is larger than 12. After all, other leaders (such as Sunday school class teachers) keep control of much larger groups. Rather, the problem comes in because the group dynamic begins to change once you get about a dozen members. The reason for this is simple: people are different.

Extroverts are energized by people. They are revitalized after an evening together at a social event. They are especially excited to get up in the morning when they know they will be with a group sometime during the day. On the other hand, introverts lose energy being with people. They are not necessarily timid or shy. Rather, they just become drained when they are with larger groups. One personality type, extrovert or introvert, is not better than another; they are just different. But as a result of this difference, when the CareRing gets above 12, the extroverts consider this larger group exciting and see the others as an audience, while the introverts become more quiet and withdrawn due to being de-energized by the group. An imbalance results in which some group members will speak more while others tone down their conversation. This difference only makes it more difficult to manage the larger a group grows.

Make it possible for your Shepherd-Leaders to lead effective groups. See that they are training apprentice leaders. And then when a group gets to about a dozen, help the group to multiply into two, with the apprentice leader taking on the role of Shepherd for one of the groups (more about how this is done in Chapter 12).

The District Coach's Span of Care

While the leader's maximum span of care is 1:12, the district coach's maximum span of care is much smaller—just 1:5. Experience has taught me the wisdom of this guideline.

Any one district coach can effectively care for and nurture only up to about five group leaders.

Over the past ten years or so, I have often wondered why some district huddles grow rapidly and others do not. It has intrigued me that a district huddle of two or three groups will grow quickly to four and five groups, while that same district huddle with the same leaders will then seldom grow to six or seven groups. In other words, smaller district huddles grow faster than larger ones.

It seems that any one district coach can effectively care for and nurture only up to about five group leaders. Any more than that and a district coach is spending all of his or her time keeping everything in place in the existing groups and can no longer concentrate on birthing new groups. In other words, they are stuck in maintenance mode and can no longer be leaders for growth. So that's why it's important to stick to the 1:5 ratio as a maximum.

When a district huddle reaches four CareRings, challenge that district coach to find an apprentice coach. As the apprentice is mentored by the district coach, that person will be prepared to take charge of CareRings on his or her own once the district huddle has six CareRings and forms two districts. And so the growing goes on.

The Small Group Pastor's Span of Care

> *Even a full-time small group pastor cannot effectively lead more than ten district coaches.*

While many can readily see the wisdom in limiting the number of persons in the care of Shepherds and district coaches, they may overlook the fact that the small group pastor can become overburdened in just the same way. Through experience, I have learned that even a full-time small group pastor cannot effectively lead more than ten district coaches while effectively building up those district huddles. The pastor may be organized, highly motivated and even visionary, but he or she cannot be effective with more than about ten district huddles. It's just the same as with the district coach: given too much responsibility the pastor will go into maintenance mode and stop being a leader for growth.

A church that grows beyond ten huddles will have to think about enlarging its pastoral staff for small groups. One option would be to hire an additional small group pastor, either part-time or full-time. Another option would be to hire assistants to work with the small group pastor.

As with any of the other spans of care, when the small group pastor's ratio is exceeded without putting a plan in place to meet personal and group needs in a constructive manner, the result inevitably places a lid on growth. The ratios are the limits of organization and care with growth. This one principle alone may well determine the difference between a ministry that stays the same year after year and one in which new people are reached and the organization is continually expanded to meet the growing demands.

LEADERSHIP MEETINGS: KEEPING THE UNITY INTACT

Call it rallying the troops. Call it keeping connected. Call it whatever you like, but don't overlook your need to get your CareRing Shepherds together on a regular basis for inspiration, training, mutual encouragement, spiritual feeding and evaluation of what you're accomplishing together. If you're a pastor in charge of the CareRings in your church, you should look at your leaders as the ones who are making it all happen. Time spent building them up is time well spent. Leadership meetings enable you to keep moving forward as one body.

I recommend three levels of regular CareRing leadership gatherings: leadership summits (all CareRing Shepherds from hosts, assistant leaders on up, led by the CareRings pastor), district coaches' team meetings (all district coaches and apprentice coaches, led by the CareRings pastor), and district huddles (all hosts and leaders and apprentice leaders within one huddle, led by the huddle's coach).

Leadership Summits

On a quarterly basis, get all Shepherd-Leaders, of whatever level, together in one place to talk about what's been happening and what's going to happen in the CareRing ministry. If you meet more frequently than quarterly, you may get complaints that it's a burden on people's schedules. Less frequently than quarterly, you risk losing the cohesion within your leadership team. Vision leaks and must regularly be restated to your whole leadership team.

The head of your church's CareRing ministry should take charge of this quarterly summit. He or she may want to have a somewhat different agenda each time. But standard features of these summit meetings may include praise reports from each huddle, announcements about recent developments in the ministry, training led by some of the more experienced leaders, a meal shared together and worship. You want all the CareRing Shepherds to leave these summits feeling pumped up about the importance of this ministry, knowledgeable about what they're supposed to do and confident that they can be successful in their own roles. An example of a recent summit is found on page 118.

WELCOME TO OUR ...

SMALL GROUPS'
LEADERSHIP SUMMIT

(Date here)

Welcome and Prayer   6:30 p.m.
  – Pastor Dave

MENU
A great meal from some of
the best cooks in the world ... YOU!
CareRing)   (This month we had a potluck meal.)

Announcements & Introductions

• Awards
• 100% District/s _____
• Welcome to new Shepherds
• Leaders:_____
• Welcome to new Apprentices:

Hot New Items ...

Welcome to new District Shepherds:
_____

THIS SUMMIT'S EVENTS
Sharing Great "Life-Changing" Praise
Reports and Powerful Ideas for Leading
Groups ... our District Shepherds (take
notes, if you like, to use in leading

Jim & Bev Cole:
Ken & Donnis Cunningham:
Gary & Gay Moore:
Troy & Koni Manzi:
Ben & Amy Kraft:
Peg Roark:
Jim Tittel:

District Coaches' Meetings and Mentoring

More than any other members of the ministry, the district coaches hold the key to effective communication and leadership. While absolutely every person matters and every role is important, your CareRing ministry will rely more on the district coach than on any others. That's why it's so important for the small group pastor to meet with the district coaches regularly apart from the quarterly leadership summits.

I recommend a monthly district coach team meeting held for about an hour and a half over a meal. This gives the pastor a chance to hear from the district coaches, to focus on current emphasis and to share from the heart. The group can also offer praise reports at this time. If a particular district coach is facing a problem, he or she can seek the counsel of the others at the meeting. They can also encourage one another and spend time in prayer

> *Even more important than these quarterly team meetings is the one-on-one mentoring that goes on between the pastor and a district coach.*

together. We also share new ideas, resources and audio tapes from time to time.

Perhaps even more important than these quarterly team meetings is the one-on-one mentoring that goes on between the pastor and a district coach. For this purpose, it helps if the pastor occasionally observes the district coach in action. By sitting in on a district huddle led by a district coach, for example, the pastor can get a better sense of the district coach's strengths and weaknesses and the problems this leader is facing.

Here are some of the ways I stay personally in touch with each district coach in my church: I make it a point to be on constant watch for significant events in their lives or needs they have; I often write a card of encouragement or a get-well card when they're sick; then, whenever possible, we get together socially. I want to build a personal friendship as well as a strong working relationship with them.

Whether in meetings or in one-on-one sessions, the emphasis is on quality care and leadership. I strive to convey the love I want them to pass on to their CareRing Shepherds. I work at modeling the same shepherding skills I desire them to develop with the leaders who serve with them.

District Huddles

A CareRing ministry gives district coaches direct responsibility for their huddles. So when it comes to district coaches exercising leadership over their CareRing Shepherds, they can do as they see fit. I recommend a monthly meeting, called a "district huddle," attended by all leaders, apprentices and hosts. But the district coaches can choose a day, place and time that is best for their particular huddle. They can approach their leaders with a style that fits them best.

For example, we call our young singles huddle and class "Gen Cross" (a play on "Gen X"). This huddle ministers to singles between the ages of eighteen and thirty, mostly in their young twenties. Then there is the "Motivator Class" district huddle for those in their sixties. These two huddles function so differently that it is almost humorous. The "Gen Cross" huddle starts its huddles with lots of loud "alternative" music; the Motivators choose an old praise chorus every time. One is loosely organized; the other is so tight it squeaks. One is laid back and casual; the other is more straight and orderly. The great advantage in giving leadership of each of these groups to their respective district coaches is obvious: they can lead in a way that fits them best.

Another advantage is that this schedule develops strong district coaches. They are seen by their leaders as "the" leader of that huddle. They are in charge of that time. The small group pastor need provide only the general guidelines as to what the elements in the huddle should be.

Then, too, district huddles allow each huddle to build on its strengths and work on the weaknesses that are unique to that particular age group. One subject that needs regular attention among our young-married adult huddle is child care. On the other hand, how to work with teenagers and respond to their craziness is a common topic of discussion among the middle adults. Again, each huddle can respond to the felt needs of that particular group of people. If the people of a given group are having trouble reaching out and opening up to new people, that need can also be addressed within the huddle.

> *Each huddle can respond to the felt needs of that particular group of people.*

Chapter Eight:
First Steps: How to Get a CareRing Started

During World War II, Beryl was going through a difficult divorce at the same time she was getting ready to give birth to a baby. It was a fearful and discouraging time for her. Beryl was then working in a factory near San Francisco, and she told her troubles to a coworker, Esther. Esther invited Beryl into her home with some other friends for a time of Bible study, prayer and fellowship.

Not being a Christian, Beryl wasn't sure she wanted to accept this invitation, but in the end she decided to go to the meeting. Later she said that she couldn't get over the joy these people had and the love they showed toward one another. She wanted what they had. So when Esther invited her to church, Beryl went and was marvelously saved.

The reason this story is significant to me is that Beryl is my mom. I was the baby who was given birth to by a mother who had fallen in love with God. From my earliest days, I watched my mother's godly life, heard her sing praises to the Lord and listened to her pray. Never once have I seen her disgrace God's name or the reputation of Christ. And it all began back in that little home prayer meeting. I have a spiritual heritage because someone cared, because the love of God was active in people's lives and because Esther Croy brought my mom into her fellowship. You would not be reading this today if it had not been for that "CareRing"!

Do you want to have a small group that sets off chain reactions of grace? This chapter will tell you how to begin.

BUILDING BLOCKS FOR STARTING SMALL GROUPS

Many times I have read a manual or book with a chapter much like this one, detailing steps to put a new ministry into place. And many times I have followed the process one step at a time as prescribed, only to fail miserably. I believe my failure was due to two reasons:

First, I had not secured God's blessings on the ministry. (Actually, more often than not, my work was really just a project of my own choosing, not a true ministry impressed on me by God.) Second, the steps in the book were too rigid and too specific. The book listed the parts of the process God had used elsewhere, but God's working in another place did not mean the same process would work for me.

Communities, churches and individuals are all different in each place where a ministry is implemented. So while we must get a clear picture of the concepts and some guidelines for how to go about it, we must leave the rest up to God. Therefore, I have chosen to give you some principles of beginning the work rather than trying to outline the 30 steps we took at such-and-such a church.

The wonderful thing about CareRings is that pastors are finding the groups help them personalize their ministry in all their various circumstances. Every church is different, and you must allow God to lead you in the particular situation in which you find yourself. If yours is a small congregation, for example, start with one group and a few leaders, build it, multiply groups and then add events and leadership as needed.

> *The wonderful thing about CareRings is that pastors are finding the groups help them personalize their ministry in all their various circumstances.*

To help you in your planning, I recommend that you read *Transitioning* by Dan Southerland.[1] It tells about the processes other churches have gone through. One of these churches, for instance, is Flamingo Road Baptist Church in Fort Lauderdale, Florida. There they have effectively incorporated small groups into their Sunday school with great success, following a proven seven-step process to discover how small groups were to be implemented in their church. Your church may not come to the same conclusions as to how groups are incorporated, but *Transitioning* is an excellent guide that will help you discover what God has in store for your congregation.

Whatever decisions you make, be clear about them. Fuzzy vision produces casual commitment. In other words, you need to agree upon the direction you will take your small group ministry. The clearer the vision, the more likely you will be to rally the involvement of your people. A clear and passionate vision

> *Fuzzy vision produces casual commitment.*

will inspire and motivate people to be a part. People will only become a part when they know this is a cause that truly matters.

Realize that small groups may be a ministry to which God is calling you and some others but not everyone in your congregation. Then again, this may be the beginning of a new day for your Sunday school and fellowship as a whole. The key is to seek God's will.

Also, try to discern God's leadership as to whether yours is to be a church *of* groups or a church *with* groups. The difference is that a church of groups involves absolutely everyone in groups. Whether you have been there 30 years or arrived last Sunday, you are asked and expected to belong to a CareRing of some type. In a church with groups, they are a major part of the life of that fellowship, but groups are only one of a number of ministries available to the people of that congregation.

When you have laid out the plan God has given you for starting CareRings in your church, take potential leaders through training. Use the CareRing Training Seminar Workbook, available from the author, for this purpose. It is filled with dozens of creative ideas you can use to train your leaders.

If you do not have leaders with experience leading small groups, you will want to bring them personally into a group first and gather them around you to watch as you model leadership for them. Just because a person has taught a Sunday school class or served on the church board does not automatically mean he or she knows how to lead a CareRing. You'll have to do training. If you do have people with experience leading groups, you are one step ahead.

In the spirit of providing adaptable guidelines instead of hard-and-fast principles, here are six building blocks with which I have built groups in three congregations.

Building Block 1: Pray for divine direction about how to begin.

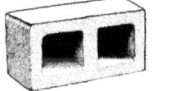 Seek God's leadership and confirmation in your own heart. Far too many churches started something because they were inspired by what happened elsewhere, only to see it crash and burn in their own context. The problem was that they had imported someone else's program rather than making it a ministry that was right for them.

This is not to say you won't use much, perhaps even all, of the material and ideas discussed here. Just be sure not to automatically start and do everything as outlined here. Let God guide you in it. Read another book or two on the subject and seek the Lord's leadership.

Building Block 2: Know where you're headed, but stay flexible. It 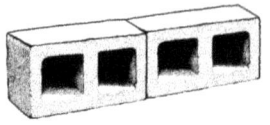 is important to know where you are headed and have some idea of how to get there. Yet, if you are sure of the way you want the groups to go, you don't need to be dogmatic about most things. While you can guide, inform and lead your people to start groups in the best ways you know how, those involved must have a sense of ownership too. So you'll want them to be a part of the decision-making process.

The problem is to know where to give in to the ideas of others and where to resist them. Sometimes lay leaders will have ideas that can cause disaster if put into practice. I saw an illustration of this in a church where I served some years ago. There were three or four laypeople who wanted to start CareRings that met only once a month. At the time I thought it was a mistake to meet so infrequently. But I wanted to be flexible, so I went along with their plan and they started out with their once-a-month groups. A year later, not one of those groups was still in existence.

Being flexible is good, but too much flexibility leaves us limp. I should not have been so flexible on the frequency of the groups. Bi-weekly groups may work in a few situations, but monthly groups definitely do not work. It's impossible to sustain momentum and cohesion when meeting that infrequently. Now I always encourage groups to meet weekly if they want to stay healthy.

> *Monthly groups definitely do not work. It's impossible to sustain momentum and cohesion when meeting that infrequently.*

In other areas, though, flexibility is a great asset. For instance, it can pay to be flexible in scheduling your leadership training sessions. In one church I offered training two or three times within a single month to make it easier for everyone to take part. It worked. We finished the first full round of training with 22 group leaders trained (out of a church of 400) by the end of the month. That's not a bad core of trained leaders!

Building Block 3: Make a list of those who might be interested.
There are dozens of ways the Holy Spirit can lead you to just the right

people who may want to be involved. It will take some patience and perhaps some searching on your part to find and involve those whom God is preparing. But trust him. The Lord knows each person's heart and can bring them to you if you can't find them.

Here are some ways to start: Think of those who have expressed an interest in growing spiritually. Try to remember if anyone has commented to you recently about needing to be involved in people's lives. Let your imagination run. Ask God to lead you to those who want to have a greater influence on other's lives. See if you can recall a conversation with another Christian who said positive things about a message or Sunday school lesson and who wished he or she had more time to explore it.

> Ask God to lead you to those who want to have a greater influence on other's lives.

Those are the kind of people you're looking for, that God may bring to you. Some of them will be participants and some will be leaders. There are a few who will see themselves as only participants at first but who, if given a chance, have the ability and spiritual commitment to eventually become leaders.

Another way to find people is with a survey identifying topics and issues in which people are interested. You can also ask for those who have had experience leading, hosting or helping lead groups to identify themselves.

Building Block 4: Share your vision as God gives you
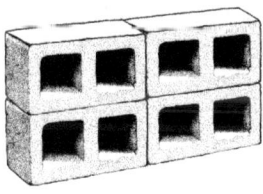
opportunities. Let interest grow naturally. Keep moving toward the goal and faithfully pass the concepts on. As you share the dream let people catch it and spontaneously respond to it. One of the best approaches is to illustrate to your friends and church family the needs CareRings will meet. As others mention their desires or needs mentioned in Building Block 3 above, share with them how you see small groups dealing with those concerns.

Building Block 5: Pray that God will give you an apprentice leader. 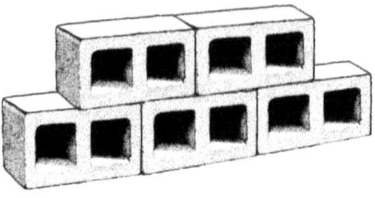 Since this is the Lord's work, he is fully able to give you the leaders and workers you need. I made finding our district coaches strictly a matter of prayer and sought guidance for weeks before God impressed upon me that it was time to talk with people about it. Of the first five couples I talked with, four of them accepted the challenge! That was a God thing!

When you find someone to serve with you, you will bring that person alongside yourself as a "Timothy." This person will catch the vision from you and work alongside you as a helper.

> *Of the first five couples I talked with, four of them accepted the challenge!*

Building Block 6: Announce when and where the CareRing will begin.  This doesn't need to be a public announcement. Instead, you can pass the news along by word of mouth to those who you think are good candidates for joining. When you invite people whom God has laid on your heart, you can tell them you have prayed and felt the way clear to invite them.

One word of caution here: Never let them hear you saying (or implying) that God told you they *should* be a part of the group. That's between God and them. But you can invite them and assure them of your confidence that God is doing a great thing in the group. When you are confident they are personally interested, you can also let them know this will need to be a priority in their lives. This may reduce the number who may think they want to be involved in the group but will realize later that the commitment is too great.

It's better with CareRings if they develop naturally. There may be two or three groups that form at the same time, and that's better than starting with only one. But remember, even Jesus started with only one small group. Remember, too, that even he did not succeed with everybody. Don't allow setbacks to stop you and don't take it personally. If CareRings are of God, people will know all about them and come in his time. If they aren't for you, no amount of coaxing, prodding or urging will make people come.

THE KICKOFF AS A SOCIAL GATHERING

One of the best ways to get many people interested in a CareRing is to make a social gathering one of your first major events. Everyone likes a party! It's relatively easy to manage. You and the other two or three people who will start your CareRing should bring any friends you know to the fun event. Be sure you are up front with guests about the purpose for the get-together, saying something like, "We're thinking about getting a few friends together for a little Bible study, and we are having them over to our house Friday for refreshments to visit about it."

Your objective for that evening is threefold:

1. You want to help the group members begin to get to know each other.

2. You want to share the vision and get them to think about being part of your dream of a group where you can share your needs, encourage one another and build one another up in love.

3. Finally, you want to discover an evening and time that might work for most of them and secure at least a tentative commitment from them to be a part. Ask them to try it for two or three weeks to see if this might be something that would help them grow.

Within two to three days after the social gathering, call the guests or set up a time to visit further with each person or couple. Share your excitement and extend a personal invitation for them to be a part. Hopefully, you can secure a commitment from them at this time. This follow-up is very important because people are busy today. Even though an invitation is worthwhile, they often forget. It's not that they don't care or can't remember; it is simply that they get busy. The personal touch of a follow-up call means a lot to people and helps get them back on track to attend.

THE FIRST REGULAR MEETING

You've decided that God is calling you to start a CareRing. You've gotten one or more people to help you. You've held a social gathering to raise interest and have personally invited several individuals to attend.

Now it's time for your first regular meeting of the CareRing. What's going to happen there? Beginnings are precious times, and so it's important to have a strong, positive first session.

In a sense, this first session is like any of the sessions that will come after. It will include the usual elements of Bible application, prayer and fellowship. So one of the things you'll want to do for the first session is make sure that you're prepared to lead an excellent Bible application, prayer and fellowship. You'll want to make a good first impression and try to see that people leave thinking, *That was really good. I'll have to come back next week.*

> *See that people leave thinking. "That was really good. I'll have to come back next week."*

Since this is all new to your group members, at each stage of the session explain what's going on. For example, before starting the Bible study and application segment, explain that you are not the "teacher" and that this is not a Sunday school class. As you approach the prayer dialogue, briefly explain how you'll go about it and why you pray this way.

In another sense, of course, the first session is unique. You need to make sure people understand what the purpose for the group is. So, at the start of the session, share your vision for the CareRing with the group. Tell them that the group's purpose is to grow spiritually and reach others. Let them know that you are available to them as a friend and a spiritual shepherd. Tell the group you believe that this is the beginning of deeper friendships and maturing faith.

Beyond these ideas, let's discuss three more suggestions for what you should say and do in connection with your first regular session:

1. Ask members to make the group a priority.

2. Lay out the five basic ground rules.

3. Get feedback from the participants.

Ask Participants to Make the Group a Priority

Normally, at the end of the meeting, people will comment about the group's value and how worthwhile it is. Seize this opportunity to encourage them to make the CareRing a priority and to treat the meeting time just like they would a doctor's appointment or an important date with their spouse. If they receive another invitation, they should explain that they are committed on that evening. Let participants know, too, that if sickness or work keeps one spouse from coming, the other spouse is still welcome. If neither can come, they should let you know in advance.

Remind your CareRing members that the busier their weeks, the greater is their need for this type of spiritual setting. Even if they miss a week, urge them to come the following week. The longer we get out of a habit (even a good one), the harder it is to get started again.

And while you're encouraging group members to make the CareRing a priority in their schedule, also encourage them to make prayer for the CareRing a priority. Even if the group members have only a few minutes a day for prayer, challenge them to take it. In fact, if they are willing to have the group hold them accountable, this can serve as a strong motivation to be consistent in prayer, Bible reading, journaling and so on.

One of the best ways to keep prayer significant is to ask the CareRing participants to pray for specific needs shared during the course of the meeting. Let them know that next week the group will be counting on hearing what God is doing. For many, this will be like living in a new world. Many people do not recognize their needs, but they hurt, are lonely, carry a burden or loss, etc., and they have nobody with whom to share the need. This support will be the means of growing loyalty to the group, so it needs to start at the beginning.

Lay Out the Five Ground Rules

As you may have gathered, this first meeting is the most crucial. How you go about it will set the tone for the rest of your sessions together. To make it go smoother, let people know the do's and don'ts:

1. ***Discussion of politics or doctrine is not allowed.*** These two subjects involve deep opinions; therefore, they tend to be divisive. A CareRing, in contrast, is committed to unity. So never allow discussion of doctrinal issues unless they are specific to the Bible application and do not reflect on anyone or any

denomination. Never get into political discussion either; there's no need for it and it can divide the group.

2. ***Self-disclosures are to be kept confidential.*** Assure the group members you will never share personal information from the CareRing with outsiders, and ask for their assurance of maintaining the same confidentiality. The one thing that will keep people away from your CareRing is for them to hear something they volunteered at the meeting being discussed elsewhere. So be intentionally and intently concerned about building trust. Never discuss something from the group with another—never!

3. ***Clearly explain prayer dialogue.*** Only one person prays at a time, but everyone is welcome to pray. Listen to God for his prompting when no one is praying, and let him bring things to mind. Never pray more than two or three sentences at a time. Usually pray for one need, or offer one item of praise, each time you pray. Pray as many times as you like, with others praying between your prayers. We do not use "Prayer Requests" because it is too easy to get sidetracked into discussion and it takes time away from prayer. Still, we encourage everyone to respond in prayer immediately to a need someone else just prayed about. We do that in prayer, not conversation!

4. ***No one is to "confess" or pray for another's faults.*** It is easy for us to tell something about a person or sensitive situation under the pretext of concern—even Christian concern. Confessing another person's faults or needs is not an appropriate CareRing activity, even as a prayer concern. Use first-person singular pronouns—*I, me, my* and so on—so that you pray on your own behalf and not on behalf of others.

5. ***All are to help produce growth.*** The vision for the group includes growing and birthing new groups. The group members should be thinking about who they can invite to the group. And they should expect to regularly pray that God will bring new people into the CareRing and raise up new leaders so that an additional CareRing can be started when the time for multiplication has come.

Get Feedback From the Participants

It can be scary to ask others to evaluate your performance in any area of life. This is equally true of your performance as a CareRing Shepherd. But if you care more for improving your ministry effectiveness than you do for your personal pride or comfort, you'll want to learn the opinions of others about the session in general and about your performance in particular.

After the first meeting, be sure to touch base with each CareRing member who was present. You don't need to do it while they are still mingling at the meeting place. But do it soon. And do it face-to-face, if possible. Perhaps you will run into some group members at church, or you can drop by their homes. Then just ask for their honest evaluation of what went on.

Really listen to their response. Listen also for what they *don't* say. The tone in their voice, their gestures and so on all communicate feelings and attitudes.

Be ready for some people to be reluctant to respond. Let them know how seriously you want to know what they thought. Be ready also for some negative feedback. Don't let that discourage you. Let them know you love them and ask them to stick with it for a few weeks—at least a month. Meanwhile, begin thinking about what you can do better next time.

THE IMPORTANCE OF PERSEVERANCE

All groups take a period of time to solidify. In fact, you should expect at least six months to pass before all the bugs are worked out, your group falls into a predictable pattern and the situation becomes stable. Be patient. Keep working at developing your group. Good things take time.

The phases before stability. Before you reach the point of stability, your group may pass through three initial phases.

The first initial phase might be called *acquaintance*. In this phase people are greeting one another politely and talking together graciously. Everybody is putting their best foot forward as they get to know each other. They are sharing only their surface problems, choosing to keep the really serious issues in their lives to themselves until they feel more comfortable with the group.

This first initial phase is natural and to be expected. Don't push people to open up so quickly that you make them uncomfortable. But gently nudge them toward greater self-disclosure and authenticity with each other by modeling such behavior yourself.

The second initial phase could be called *misunderstanding*. It is one in which some people begin opening up more and others surface as "problem solvers." They will answer someone's need with a story of how they solved that problem. They will directly tell them not to be discouraged or upset. This may or may not be helpful.

When this happens, let everyone know it is fine for a group member to be angry or upset about what has gone on in his or her life. Encourage that member to go on telling about his or her feelings. What you are doing is giving space for ventilating emotions. You are allowing anyone to share what's on their heart, knowing the group can hear it and continue to love them.

The third initial phase could be called *chaos*. In this phase it seems that each person has his or her own agenda for the group. Some may even have a strategy for exerting power over the direction the group goes in. Not all of this may be expressed openly, but you can detect it beneath what people are doing and how they are acting. There can be confusion and hurt feelings and some may be ready to bail from the group.

If your group passes through this phase, don't be frightened but submit your concerns to God privately. Trust him to bring order out of chaos (he can, you know!). Meanwhile, quietly and gently go about exerting your authority as a leader to do with your group what you believe God would have you to do.

Once you have passed successfully through these three initial phases, your group should begin to enjoy the closeness and the trust that are the rewards of a good small group.

What happens when new people join. Of course, whenever you add a new group member, you'll have to go through the process of building trust all over again. Some have been hurt and disillusioned in the past. In some cases, people have been taken advantage of, taken for granted or taken in by some "Christian" who turned out to be using them. In other cases, they came to believe God had let them down. They prayed for something and he didn't give it to them as they believed they deserved. Whatever the case, people need time to rebuild trust. Their faith in others was bruised and healing takes time. (Again, for this reason, be sure to hold discussions in confidence.)

Typically, however, you will notice people becoming more open after about three to four weeks. Don't be discouraged if it takes longer. In the men's small group I started in Texas, we met a full eight months before one of the men shared a personal need in his own life.

Small groups are like marriages in many ways. They are based on love. It takes a deep commitment to get them going well. And there is always a "honeymoon" period. But, as in a marriage, nothing is more exciting and worthwhile than bringing new "spiritual children" into the home. Couples—and CareRings—come alive when someone new comes to the home! It seems that procreation is why we were created. That is also true in the Christian fellowship—we were saved to serve, and we serve to save others.

> *Small groups are like marriages in many ways. ... It takes a deep commitment to get them going well.*

GROWTH AND NONGROWTH

We never know quite what to expect when we embark on this adventure in caring. The most important thing is to set out and lead for God and others. If you succeed, it will be because of him. If you fail, don't let it be because you have not been faithful. It is important that you set your sights now and stay on the course that will get you there. Just be about the Father's business. Leave the results with him. Right now, plan that, whether you are effective or not, you will know you have not been a failure.

A few years ago, Bill and Carol accepted the challenge of shepherding a new group. They took training and began inviting their friends to establish a new CareRing. One by one, their friends agreed with the cause, said they would pray about being a part and did not join. Bill and Carol had been enthusiastic and optimistic. They seemingly did everything right. They couldn't form a group, but they didn't quit.

We visited about it and prayed a few more weeks. They caught a renewed vision and once again began telling their friends about the possibility of a new group. This time the outcome was totally different. One by one, their acquaintances accepted their invitation. They found an apprentice and began their group. They were elated, to say the least. Within six months, their apprentice started a new CareRing, and there were almost 30 people being loved, encouraged and nourished spiritually from Bill and Carol's original group. If they had not gone on, if they had given in to their initial discouragement, those CareRings would not be in existence today and those 30 people would not have a community.

Both growth and nongrowth present challenges small group leaders must face wisely.

What to Do When Your Group Doesn't Grow

I sincerely believe that virtually anyone who carefully follows the tested and time-proven concepts in this book will eventually be effective at leading small groups. However, we cannot control these things. It is fully possible that you may not be effective for some unidentified reason.

Clearly, groups are a concept as old as the Bible and have been a means throughout history of reaching lost, hurting people. Yet in some given situation it may not click. What do you do in such a situation? Nothing. Don't throw away your faith. Don't conclude that groups are not of God. Just know you have done your best, and trust God with the rest.

However, speaking from my 14 years of experience with groups, I can testify that no leader I worked with personally and who followed what I have outlined here has failed. Not one! We can do one thing for sure—plan to be effective. Learn the material well and follow it until you find some variation that works better.

Good prevention is better than excellent cure. Here are four preventative steps we can take:

> *Good prevention is better than excellent cure.*

1. ***Pray for growth.*** Dare to believe God is in your ministry and that he wants you to be effective. Nothing of lasting value ever happens other than God's work. He is our source and our resource. So first of all pray, believing that God wants you to minister to those in need. As you begin, make sure you add feet to your faith. Anything new takes more energy and commitment than maintaining the status quo. It will mean praying as though it all depended on God and working as though it all depended on you. The only reason our work is important is that God works through people. Our work will consist of staying in touch with

people through the decision-making process. We don't want to bother them but rather to make them feel welcome and wanted.

2. ***Keep the empty chair visible.*** Specifically, ask members during prayer time who they are planning to invite. Then pray for those people by name. Make outreach and evangelism clearly a part of your purpose. Ask God to give you a burden for lost people and to bring them across your path.

3. ***Be optimistic yet realistic.*** Life, being what it is, will bring evenings that are difficult. There will be people who say they will come and don't. They may even apologize and promise to be there next week, only to be absent again. Remember, this is God's work. You are not doing this for big numbers anyway. If you can help even a half dozen people, it will be worth any amount of effort you put into it. Many groups have become strong once they started enthusiastically with those they had and let God make some major differences in their lives. Word got out and there were more wanting to come than could be easily accommodated.

4. ***Ask for feedback.*** Find an individual or a couple who will be open and honest. Ask what their appraisal of the group is and really listen. Many times a problem is minor and can easily be solved, once we know what it is. People hesitate to provide feedback for fear they will hurt our feelings. But if we take the initiative, they will tell us. Problems are simple to correct if, for example, the meetings are too long, if someone is dominating the conversation or if the couple just doesn't feel they fit the group. Shorten the meetings; talk to the vocal person; help the couple locate a group in which they would belong. Then do whatever you can to clear up misunderstandings or solve problems. Sometimes a new night, a different home or different child care arrangements can solve it all.

What to Do When Your Group Does Grow

Sometimes it is hard to handle growth. We can get caught up with pride, believing that somehow we have done it. But if you approach your small group as a ministry, then God is the one who makes it effective. Never us.

> *If you approach your small group as a ministry, then God is the one who makes it effective.*

There are at least three things to determine now that you will do in a growth situation.

1. ***Thank God for the growth.*** If God blesses (and he surely can), keep the work in his hands. Thank him personally and publicly for what he has done. Resolve in your heart that you will keep this ministry in his hands.

2. ***Train an apprentice leader.*** The way to do this is to be on the lookout for people who may have the potential to be apprentices. Be watching early on for those who comment about how helpful the group is to them. Be ready to follow up immediately with the invitation to pray the closing prayer the next week, lead the ice-breaker at the beginning of the following meeting or read Scripture at the next week's CareRing. When they agree, you know you are sure to have them back (we will always attend something of which we are a part). You may even get two or three immediately involved in this way. Then, after they have helped in those ways for a couple of months, watch for effectiveness. Notice that when one of the potential apprentices prays, there is a unique spirit in the room, or that when one opens the meeting with some brief type of discussion starter, people really come together. Let God guide you to people he may be preparing for leadership. If you feel so led, invite one or more of them to begin thinking about helping you out more frequently and later ask them about being an apprentice. Let it grow naturally.

3. ***Begin preparing to multiply your group.*** Talk about this goal early on with your group. In fact, it's best to make it clear from the start that the group is for God, not for yourselves. This is one way to be proactive, reaching out to others around you and

trying to impact them for Jesus. And continually remind your members of your purpose to reach others—that is, to start new groups.

The sign of a healthy body is that cells are multiplying. It's the same in a small group ministry. Multiplication is the ultimate success you look forward to when you start a small group ministry. Pray for it, work for it and celebrate it when it comes.

As soon as your CareRing reaches 14 in attendance more than two weeks in a row, make plans to multiply. Work with your apprentice leader and any others who have shown leadership to get a second group under way.

Thus, the process of taking first steps starts all over again.

> *Multiplication is the ultimate success you look forward to when you start a small group ministry.*

Chapter Nine:
Decisions, Decisions: Major Choices You Must Make as You Start Out

*T*he three times I have helped start a small group ministry in a church as a staff member, we began each one differently than we did the others. In my Texas pastorate, it was a men's group that we started first. Later, others in the church became interested in the idea and started different types of groups. When I was on staff at First Nazarene in Nashville, we started with eight groups associated with the Sunday school. But then, within the first year, we realized that we needed to add six more. At Trevecca Community Church of the Nazarene, where I served on the staff as discipleship pastor, we started with four groups and they were all organized differently.

This variety of approaches in starting small groups is not all bad. After all, every situation is different, with different needs and different gifts among the leadership given by God to meet those needs. On the other hand, I have learned some lessons along the way that I like to pass along to others so that they don't have to make the same mistakes I did. One lesson is that you should make certain crucial decisions up front so that you don't get yourself into a mess that you have to clean up later. The previous two chapters should have made it clear what some of those early decisions are (how large to let groups grow before dividing, what objectives to have for a first regular session, and so on). But there are at least a trio of other decisions you should know about.

This chapter presents three questions you should ask yourself at the outset of your CareRing ministry. (1) *What does the first year of a CareRings ministry look like?* (2) *Which model should we follow in starting our ministry?* (3) *What else are we going to have to give up so that we have time for small groups?* It may be that no two churches will answer these questions exactly the same way. But certainly no church should neglect to consider them.

WHAT DOES THE FIRST YEAR LOOK LIKE?

Let's take an imaginary walk through the first year of a small group ministry in a local church. You may not want to start your CareRings in the same way, but it can be helpful to imagine how others do it.

First Church of the Imagination

In this imaginary church the pastor and staff have come to see how powerful small groups can be, so they decide to begin sharing their vision with key players in the church. They meet with the main lay leadership body of the church and try to communicate what groups will and will not do. They spell out how the groups might build community, the ways they can be used to build leadership into the people and why it is so essential that everyone commit to the ministry.

At that point all the leaders decide whether the primary focus of their ministry will be outreach and evangelism or the folding of new members into the fellowship and assimilating them into the body. This is an important step. Much of what you do to start and build the ministry depends on this decision. Then you may decide to do both outreach and community development.

Now, the pastor gets the CareRings ministry under way in the simplest way possible by just beginning a group himself. He starts by looking for the most teachable, influential group of people he knows. He talks with them personally to share the vision and get them together for a social time in which they form a group together. When they get together he secures their commitment once he sees excitement building. They set a date to start the CareRing, pray together and select a subject to begin studying.

As the CareRing gets under way, the pastor involves each participant weekly in some part of the meeting. He watches how they follow through, how seriously they take the task given them and how cooperative others are when they lead. All this is to see what leadership skills they have, what their weak points might be and where they need coaching. He supports them by identifying all the things they do well with specific feedback after each meeting.

When he sees some potential leaders emerging, he gives them more instructions about additional responsibility and offers them other tasks in leading the group. In short, within four to six months, the pastor has given group members the opportunity to build their confidence and has watched as they have built commitment to the group and to leading. Then he offers leadership training to the group and challenges them all to start a group within another six months.

So, in less than a year, the pastor has six to eight couples or pairs of singles ready to start their own CareRings. At this point, the ministry is launched. It is announced publicly and each couple shares the difference CareRings has made in their lives. (For this reason, it is important that the pastor has always been watching and listening for how God has moved in their lives and changed them.)

Variations on the First Year

The approach used at First Church of the Imagination is not the only one possible. There are other variations you could try.

Some pastors may opt to include Sunday school teachers and other pastoral staff in the first group. Hopefully, once they begin to see the value of the group, the other pastors and Sunday school teachers will be building interest within their areas of pastoral influence and classes. Then they are taught to look for potential leaders within their classes and challenged to start their own CareRing with that group. A district coach is selected from among these people once they have led their own CareRing effectively and have brought in new leaders themselves.

In other cases, I have seen all the leaders of a church trained at one time. Then each Sunday school class starts an initial group led by some of the people who have been through training. I have trained as many as 78 people in one day, out of a church of 250 attenders. That church started six groups two months after they took the initial training and had 14 CareRings within the first year.

If a church opts for this second approach, it is almost a necessity that they hire a consultant to walk them through the initial six months of operation. A consultant, well-versed and experienced in small group operation, should make at least two visits to the church and be available by e-mail and phone for support. His or her first visit is to present the plan to all the leaders of the church. The consultant may also do the initial training if the church is ready to make a commitment at that point. He or she should return in four to six months for a second visit to walk them through the organizational phase. Most churches can get started; keeping going is the important part.

There are a number of steps congregations may take to move into a full-scale group ministry.

1. As they have enough leaders, they can give the name of every new person or couple to a leader and have them contact the new person, inviting them to their CareRing. This can be an excellent way to assimilate new people into the fellowship and make them feel welcomed.

2. If each CareRing is started in a class, when they birth new groups, they have a ready-made pool from which to build the new group. The class members are more likely to come since they already know the new leaders from class.

Once the first few groups have started, keep your leaders in contact with one another. Actually, it is ideal to meet with all leaders (as a kind of CareRing of their own) every couple of weeks at the beginning. They can help each other solve problems and pray for one another, and the pastor can give them ongoing training so that they stay fresh. The first gathering I suggest is one with all your leaders and apprentices. When you have six groups, it's time to find two district coaches and get those groups into two huddles with three groups each. In some cases, the new huddles may be together in a Sunday school class.

When huddles are formed, each district coach will lead his or her own district huddle once a month. He or she will do the same things with them that the pastor has been doing with all the leaders before huddling took place. Some churches call the format of the huddles a "VHS." That stands for vision casting, huddling together for prayer and support.

Once momentum begins to build around the small group ministry, a regular celebration of some sort needs to be built into the schedule. Commissioning the new leaders in a public service serves to remind the congregation of the value of the ministry and importance of leading as a leader, host or district coach. It will also elevate the role these leaders play in serving the congregation and folding new people into the fellowship.

WHICH START-UP MODEL TO USE

The best way to introduce and develop CareRings is through relationships. The pastor and other staff members will identify leaders, share the initial concepts and values and provide training and leadership. However, as soon as it is presented as a "program" or "the new way we're going to fix things," it is doomed. Some of the genius and most of the strength of groups is that they are led by and for the people. As key concepts are conveyed to leaders, and as they are empowered to lead, let the ministry grow naturally from the bottom up. Let people assume leadership as soon as possible.

Having said that, let me present to you three excellent models for starting groups. Though these are not exhaustive or all-inclusive, they are three of the most common and effective ways of starting CareRings. The first is the turbo model for rapid start-up. The second is the Sunday school launch for the gradual spreading of small groups among class members. And the third is the special interest model in which church members are won over to the idea of CareRings through topical groups.

Read the description of each model and think about which might work for your situation. As always, you know your church best. The real solution is found when leaders come together, pray earnestly and discover God's solution for their fellowship.

Start-Up Model A: Turbo Groups

Looking to start your small group ministry fast? A turbo group may be the answer for you.[1]

A turbo group is a small group made up entirely of persons who are intending to lead their own groups. This group is designed to train these new leaders rapidly (hence the word "turbo"), and so it is intensive but lasts for a relatively brief period, normally from six to eight weeks. The group is led by the pastor, the small group pastor or a key lay leader dedicated to small groups. But all members share various aspects of leadership in the group.

A turbo group schedule goes something like this: Once the initial training is completed, a group forms and is conducted like any new group would be for the first three or four weeks. The main leader of the group leads those sessions. After that, a different member or couple in the group leads each week. The weekly schedule is different now, too, with half of the time spent in an accelerated CareRing session and the other half of the time spent evaluating the leader. Every evening, every activity and every question in the turbo group includes the purpose of developing leaders. So it is ideal if each evening can be scheduled to run two hours, with one hour for the regular session and one hour to discuss and evaluate the meeting. I have used the Serendipity publication *Beginnings* with great results in starting turbo groups.

When the turbo group is finished, introduce your newly trained leaders to your Sunday school classes, expressing your confidence in their ability to lead excellent small groups. Then let them arrange for host homes and get their groups started. In no time you'll have several rings of people learning more about each other and about what God wants for them than they ever imagined. Growth will happen fast if you use the turbo model.

Start-Up Model B: Sunday School Launch

A slower (but equally effective) model for start-up is the Sunday school launch. In this model you simply start one or more small groups with Sunday school class members as the participants in the group. Often leaders within your adult education program—teachers, assistant teachers, greeters and so on—are good candidates for participation in these early groups. They are the most committed people you have and comprise a pool of your most likely future small group leaders.

The number of groups you can start at the beginning is determined by the number of trained and experienced group leaders you have available. It might be just one group with one leader—you. But as the first group(s) grow, you appoint apprentice leaders, multiply cells and *voilà!* Your small group ministry is off and running. In a matter of months (or a year or two at the most) the majority of your Sunday school class members can be involved in small groups with established huddles. Your CareRing ministry will then be fully functioning as a means to grow both the Sunday school and the small groups.

There's a variation on this model to consider. In this variation, you form a small group entirely with Sunday school class greeters—the men and women who shake hands and welcome members and visitors to class on Sunday morning. By starting a small group with these people, you're ensuring that a few of them will become small group leaders themselves before long. Greeters make excellent leaders! Not only do they tend to have extroverted, caring personalities but they are in a position to invite class visitors to show up for their groups during the week. Newcomers get folded into CareRings quickly if class greeters are also small group leaders.

Regardless of who the participants in the first group(s) are, you'll soon reach a point where you have a few leaders ready to go and the CareRing ministry is poised to begin expanding. That's the point where you want to cast the vision for the small group ministry to all the adult Sunday school class members. In order to get interest, be sure to present it as the dream of the whole church leadership and as something that the class teacher and other class leaders are fully behind. Describe it as a way of getting to know one another better and providing quality care to each person. Introduce the leaders and challenge class members to give CareRings a try. Experience has proved that, once they try it, they'll love it!

If you're worried that class members may be wary of attending small groups, try this technique: use a portion of class time for small group experiences, giving class members a chance to discuss the topic of the lesson in groups of six or eight. In these class-time small groups, class members will discover that they do not know each other as well as they thought they did. This will whet their appetite for regular small group experiences during the week in CareRings. Your problem may be that you don't have enough leaders for all the class members who want to get involved in groups!

The Sunday school launch is a proven method of spreading CareRings among Sunday school classes in a natural way.

Start-Up Model C: Special Interest Groups

The third start-up model is a more indirect method than either using turbo groups or launching within the Sunday school. In this third model you get people used to attending small groups by attracting them to groups formed around topics of special interest to them. For example, you could advertise the start of a support group for parents of teenagers. Potential members for this group might be committed church members who regularly go to Sunday school, casual attenders who have never entered a Sunday school classroom or even those outside the church who happened to hear about the group. The special interest group carries on for a period of time, and then you try to persuade its participants to join a regular CareRing.

Just about any topic can work for this kind of special interest group. How about stress management? Or family budgeting? Or couples going through the post-honeymoon period? Let your imagination run. Just be sure to get an okay for the topic and materials used from the pastor or relevant church leader before you commit your CareRing to it. You may wish to choose your topic by surveying the congregation. If you want to use curriculum, Serendipity House and other publishers offer numerous topical studies for small groups.

Like any start-up model, this one has its advantages and its disadvantages. The upside of this model is that, if you choose your topic well, you can just about be guaranteed that you'll have plenty of people interested in joining. Thus, you'll be able to get many people acclimated to the small group environment. The downside is that it can be difficult to transition from this situation to a class-oriented small group ministry. After a few months together in a special interest study, people may not want to get into a CareRing associated with a particular adult Sunday school class. They will have bonded with one another and grown used to the topical approach.

But it is possible to overcome the resistance to CareRings that the special interest start-up might create. One way is to change membership in your special interest groups frequently, perhaps every six weeks or three months. In other words, plan to have your special interest groups finish their studies within a set (and relatively short) period of time, then disband them and start all new groups. At disbanding time, people might be more willing to try out a CareRing.

The special interest model may be for you if you think you're going to have to woo your church members to the small group experience over time, and if you're willing to have a slower and possibly rocky transition to a normal CareRing ministry.

TRAINING OPTIONS

Training for any start-up of CareRings at a local church–whether you use turbo groups, a Sunday school launch or special interest groups–should follow one, or a combination of the following approaches:

Option 1: Schedule a training session in which the pastor or small group pastor leads the training with the use of this book and the training materials that go along with it. This is the best option because it enables the small group pastor to create a unique and unified small group ministry for the church while establishing his or her position as the in-church expert on CareRings. (The CareRing training workbook is a compact, yet creative tool to use for this purpose. It is designed to insure there will be involvement and participation by trainees.) However, this option presupposes that the small group pastor has sufficient knowledge and experience of CareRings to do such training. If that's not the case, go to Option 2.

Option 2: Go to an outside source for training. This could mean taking your key leaders to a nearby church where training is being held, or it could mean bringing in someone to lead the training in your church. In either case, be sure the trainer thoroughly knows the CareRing material and understands the principles involved. This option is perhaps not as personalized for your church as Option 1, but it does ensure that you get quality training.

Option 3: If neither of the first two options is available, give your key players this book and its related material to read. Then schedule a Saturday morning in which to share discoveries with one another and discuss how you want it all to work in your church. Together, with God's help, you should be able to "train" each other and plan a CareRing ministry that will work. But this option should only be used if no experienced trainer is available.

WHAT TO GIVE UP?

For a long time, Oilton Christ Fellowship in Oilton, Oklahoma, has been a healthy, active church. At least 250 persons meet for worship on Sunday mornings. (Given that Oilton is a community of only 1,200 persons, that means more than one in five local citizens attends the church!) Nevertheless, this church felt the need for a small group ministry to help them go deeper in their faith and in their life together.

Pastor Bill Ryan heard about CareRings and invited me to consult with his church for six months so they could get small groups started.

I agreed, and we set the date for the initial training session with his church's leaders, including pastors, Sunday school teachers and potential CareRing Shepherds. We expected from 30 to 40 people to attend this first session. Imagine our surprise when 78 people came for training! Here was a real readiness for small groups.

Within five months, this church had six groups formed. In eight months, they had eleven. An effective CareRing ministry was well under way.

Later, during a follow-up phone conversation with the church's associate pastor, Gary Krlin, I learned that Oilton Christ Fellowship had canceled its Sunday evening services. "Why?" I asked in surprise. When I visited the church, it had seemed to me that everything was going well with that service.

Gary told me everything *had* been going well. But he added that the people loved their new groups so much that they preferred them over the Sunday evening service. Since they had limited time, they would rather set aside Sunday evening for their groups than for the service. The church leaders agreed.

Pastor Bill Ryan said, "Really, why would I not give up a service attended by 110 people and led by 15 when instead I could have 140 people ministered to in their homes with the help of 30 leaders?" He had made his point. If the choice was between a Sunday evening service and the small groups, the small groups were the better use of time.

The Christ Fellowship discovery is the rule, not the exception. For anything worthwhile, there is always a price to pay. When you start a small group ministry, plan to end some other service, program or activity of the church to give your people time to attend their small groups. Plan, also, to refocus your church leadership's energy partly away from other concerns and onto your new small group ministry.

Yes, there is a price to pay for small groups. In fact, starting a CareRing ministry is always harder than it first appears. But trust me, it's worth it!

> *For anything worthwhile, there is always a price to pay.*

Giving Up a Poorly Attended Service

Small groups are going to revolutionize your church. They're going to touch people's lives on a deeper level than almost anything else you can imagine your church doing. So is it so bad if something else—some weaker program—has to go to make room for small groups?

As in the case of Oilton Christ Fellowship, the elimination of a church service is often a good option. In reality, every church where I have ever consulted has had at least one service that was in trouble, perhaps a Wednesday evening prayer service or a Sunday evening worship service. Only a fraction of the total church body would be attending such a service, but the pastor would be reluctant to get rid of it because it was a tradition in the church or because it meant a lot to a few people. So the church would keep it going year after year, hoping it would eventually resurrect itself. But then, when the church caught on to the important role small groups were going to play in their fellowship (as well as the amount of time small groups were going to consume), they were ready—finally—to let the old service go. It has always been for the best.

In fact, there are dangers if you *don't* get rid of the weak service and put something stronger—namely, your new small group ministry in its place. If you let a weak program go on too long, people will be disappointed. And who is going to get fed up and leave first? Your strongest leaders, the ones who demand the most and give the most to the church. Some of these leaders could make small groups flourish, if approached for this purpose before they quit attending one of the weak services. Once they get out of the habit of attending, they may not want to start in a group. How much better it is to take initiative and be proactive in providing training and leadership while making plans to substitute small groups for a weaker service!

Of course, initially your church leaders may be on the receiving end of some objections about eliminating a long-standing church service. You'll want to be ready for such objections and be prepared to smooth ruffled feathers. But the increased effectiveness you will get by swapping a weak ministry for a strong one will be well worth whatever backlash you initially get. As people's lives change and your church begins to grow, the objections will fade away.

Giving Up Leadership Focus on Other Matters

It's not only rank-and-file church members who are going to have to get used to doing without something they're fond of. Church leaders (who might actually be happy about getting rid of that albatross of a Wednesday evening prayer service) are going to have to devote considerable time, thought and energy to small groups. In order to do so they're going to have to steal time, thought and energy away from other concerns.

A one time price that leaders are going to have to pay is the cost of training and leading all the new group leaders and hosts. Then there are the prices of effort, time and the need for a real focus on the vision and purpose of a CareRing ministry in your fellowship. This takes a heart-level commitment. I never advise churches to start a small group ministry unless their senior pastor, any staff and governing groups are totally committed to it. Typically, the church board, council or deacons must be in wholehearted agreement for groups to do well. But this is only the start.

> *I never advise churches to start a small group ministry unless their senior pastor, any staff and governing groups are totally committed to it.*

When you're ready to put a CareRing ministry in place, all Sunday school teachers must be informed and helped to see the value. This may also include class councils, leadership teams in adult classes and adult department leadership, if your church has them in place.

Because of such costs, the pastoral leadership of the church is going to have to make some decisions. Maybe it's time to add a new staff member. Maybe staff members are going to have to reorganize their time or eliminate some duties or activities they've gotten used to.

Whatever you do, it is simply imperative that the pastor and the people make a unilateral commitment to the value of small groups. Finding and developing new leadership, providing training and adjusting schedules will all naturally follow once the church leadership has chosen to commit to small groups.

AN ENCOURAGEMENT

In chapters seven through nine, you learned what it takes to put a CareRing ministry into place. This chapter, in particular, has shown you that you're going to have to make some tough decisions and do things differently in your church if you're going to make small groups a reality. But before we go any further, let me give you some encouragement: it's all doable and it's all worthwhile!

Many churches have preceded you in this adventure. I've worked with many of them personally and have seen how they have come through the difficult transition with flying colors, their only regret being that they didn't start sooner. They're growing and seeing lives changed to become more Christlike. Is this what you want too? Then get organized and take it step-by-step. God has, and will, bless your church with all you need to create a small group ministry that honors him.

Meanwhile, there are a few more topics to cover. In the remaining chapters we'll look at the ongoing process of leadership development and ways to keep on building your CareRing ministry and its leadership.

Chapter Ten:
Your Other Job: The Importance of Leaders Developing Leaders

*E*verybody thought Bradley was a born leader. Bradley loved people and people loved Bradley. After a long day of leading a team at work, Bradley couldn't wait to spend an evening leading his not-so-small group. He somehow commanded attention and could keep listeners interested in everything he had to say. People showed up for the group meetings largely because of the attraction of Bradley's personality. *Oh, you're in Bradley's group,* people would say. *What a great guy!*

But then Bradley got a job transfer and suddenly he was gone. His small group struggled on without him for a little while, then vanished without a whimper. Bradley may have had some of the qualities of a leader, but he fell down in one critical area: *he failed to identify and train others to lead.* Perhaps he was more interested in attracting attention toward himself than in directing attention toward God. Perhaps not. Either way, because of his failure at training others, the group couldn't survive without him.

Bradley evidently hadn't grasped the truth that every leader of a small group has two jobs. The first is leading the small group. That's obvious. But the other job—every bit as important—is raising up new leaders. Moses had Joshua. Elijah had Elisha. Paul had Timothy. Likewise, every leader in a small group ministry should be reproducing himself or herself in another. This is the apprenticeship process.

> *Every leader in a small group ministry should be reproducing himself or herself in another.*

Only this second job keeps the first job from becoming an end in itself. Only as we constantly keep before ourselves the value of training others do we keep from being the focus ourselves. Remember, the purpose of having small groups is not to have small groups. Small groups are *not* an end in themselves; they are the means to the end of reaching, loving and changing others for the sake of our Lord. Our mission is not to build *our* kingdom but to build *his* kingdom. Everything we do serves this end.

> *Our mission is not to build our kingdom but to build his kingdom. Everything we do serves this end.*

In every training session I lead, I challenge new leaders to realize up front how essential it is to reproduce themselves. For small groups to continue to be small, for new groups to be started, for us to constantly reach more and more people, we must constantly be identifying and developing new leaders. There are not many principles more necessary to catch than this one. Almost nothing matters more than this when it comes to building an aggressive small group ministry and touching your entire congregation.

In this chapter we will walk, step-by-step, through the essentials of implementing your small group leadership. We will cover numerous ideas used to find, develop and empower new group leaders and new district coaches. To some readers, more experienced in developing new leaders, these items may seem elementary. But believe me, I have watched even seasoned leaders totally miss opportunities to find and develop new leaders. So here we go. Fasten your seat belts.

NEW GROUP LEADERS

When we realize that reproducing ourselves in others has expotential implications, we begin to understand why it is so essential that we do this. It is like the difference between leading someone to Christ and raising up a witnessing Christian.

If you lead one person to Christ a day for a month, there are 31 new Christians at the end of the month. But get this: if one of us won only one person to the Lord each day for a month, and if each of those persons who accepted Christ led one person a day to the Lord for the rest of the month, by the end of one month there would be 536,870,911 new Christians.[1] That's the power of reproduction. It is mind-boggling.

Then, too, there are very few accomplishments more fulfilling than investing in a potential leader and seeing that person find his or her own place and take leadership of a group. This process is akin to seeing your children grow up to be productive and happy adults. It's exciting to realize that we have had a hand in influencing every single person ever led, taught, guided or helped by an apprentice we trained. When apprentices take hold of their own groups, we see the remarkable power of Jesus' concept of discipleship put into play. There was no way that the little band of 12 apostles Jesus left on earth when he returned to heaven could impact a pagan culture such as Rome or clear the clogged arteries of preferential treatment against Israel all on their own. Even the 120 in the upper room could not have done that alone. But when they all shared the changes in their lives with their friends and families, when they passed the Gospel on and told everyone they influenced to pass it on, the world was changed.

It is true that developing another leader for a small group is far more time consuming and intricate than just leading a group yourself. But the difference when the goal is accomplished is worth far more than the effort, patience and concentration it takes to achieve.

As I began leading the first small groups in the church I pastored in Washington with our little band of leaders, we affected perhaps 50 to 60 people. Yet when I work with leaders of the group leaders—over 50 of them—the difference is like day compared to night. In all, we have the capacity to minister to over 1,000 people and actually touch about 900 lives every week.

Your church can experience remarkable growth as well if you pay attention to finding, developing and empowering new leaders.

Finding New Group Leaders

The first, most obvious step in reproducing yourself is to identify potential leaders. We are going to cover a wide range of methods for discovering possible leaders, and we will discuss the general process through which they are selected and developed.

From the first regular meeting of the CareRing, the leader should discuss his or her vision for growth and birthing new groups. This should include a statement that everyone in the group will need to pray together that God will give the leader an assistant, who might eventually start another group. If this is clearly stated up front, most groups will accept the idea and begin praying for a helper.

There are three reasons this is so important:

- First, when the group hears the leader talk about this dream, they will share it. As they pray, they will begin to own the vision. Later, when an apprentice is identified, they will consider this new leader an answer to their prayers. It is vitally important that the dream be shared up front because, once the CareRing builds strong relationships and members bond with one another, they have reason to resist starting another group. But as they share the dream of multiplication, they can overcome this resistance in themselves.

- Second, as the group members pray for an apprentice leader, God may lay it on one of their hearts to be that person. Actually, the stronger and more mature your people are, the more likely it is they will take on leadership.

- Third, we all function better when we have a purpose. A vision is inspiring. There is something captivating and exciting about believing we are part of something greater than ourselves. Therefore, most CareRings that accept this dream will be motivated and inspired by it. As God leads group members to the future leader, they all sense that they are part of the adventure.

QUESTIONS TO ASK ABOUT POTENTIAL LEADERS

As a group leader considers individuals in the group as apprentice leaders, he or she should be asking these questions about the apprentices:

- How well do they apply what we teach in leader training?
- What people skills do they demonstrate?
- How responsive are others to their leadership? That is, do they truly influence other members of the group?
- Do they follow through? When asked the week before to do the ice-breaker, for example, are they well prepared for it?
- Do they take initiative? Whenever a need presents itself, are they the ones who fulfill it or encourage others to do so?
- What kind of attitude do they have?
- Are they part of the church family? Are they committed to the mission and membership of the church?

Beyond sharing the vision for an apprentice leader, a leader must begin actively looking for an individual who might be that leader. In the next section of this chapter, we'll look at techniques for doing just that.

Special Techniques for Finding New Group Leaders

Over my 14 years of working with churches in small group ministry, I've uncovered a number of techniques for identifying possible leaders. You may not want to use all of these techniques, but reading about them should at least get you going.

1. Observe who responds fastest to study materials. This first technique may seem a bit odd. And, of course, you can't rely on this one technique alone. But I've found that this simple behavioral test can successfully give an indication of who might be a candidate for leading a small group.

During the course of a meeting, hold out a stack of study guides or other materials that you are using to lead the group. Offer it in the center so that anyone can take it and begin passing the materials around. Then see who offers to help you first. If one person responds to this test repeatedly, it is possible that this person is a future leader. At least you know that he or she has a helpful attitude and a natural attraction to study materials.

2. Listen for offers of help. Often prospective leaders will identify themselves without even knowing it by offering to help in various ways. As a group starts, people want to help get it going. So listen carefully. In one new group, I received offers to host a CareRing, bring refreshments, make phone calls, write a reminder or thank you note and even sponsor a baby shower. Lots of potential leaders in that group!

Accept every offer you can. Then people feel a sense of ownership toward their group and feel they are valued within it. More importantly, by giving others a task, you have opened a door for them to lead.

This year at Central Community Church, one CareRing found their apprentice couple within one month of forming their group. This couple trained for one day. Then I had both the husband and wife do something every week in the group. I coached them as to what went well after each meeting, throwing in suggestions for improvement. Within seven months of starting with CareRings, this couple was leading their own group.

3. Watch for follow through and effectiveness. Perhaps no skill will help you find a new apprentice more than the ability to observe how well others do whatever they are asked to do. This takes some concentration on the part of the leader, but it is well worth the effort.

Actually, this is one of the reasons I recommend that both husband and wife share the leadership position. While one is busy leading, the other can be observing how effective people are at doing what was asked of them.

4. Look for leadership surfacing in activities. The old adage goes, "Great leaders are like cream; they always rise to the top." I don't know much about cream, but I do know how leadership works. Leaders will rise to the occasion. My friend, Bear Deardorff reminded me of this one day at a seminar.

The groups of people attending the seminar were playing an icebreaker game called "One Frog," which takes concentration and organization to win. Some groups became confused—participants had trouble communicating with each other and came close to giving up. Then Bear pointed out to me how one person in each group was asserting himself or herself. These individuals pointed to whoever was supposed to go next, kept track of everyone's place or said out loud what each participant should say as it became their turn. *There you have it,* I said to myself. *Those people are leaders.*

You can try this exercise in your small group to spot prospective leaders. Give the group a task to do together without you (perhaps play a challenging game that requires staying on track and remembering where the teams are). Then step back and see who emerges as a leader.

> *Ask a couple of group members to lead the two subgroups. This will give you a chance to observe them in leadership situations.*

Similarly, watch for potential leaders in casual social settings. Take note of how genuinely interested individuals are in others when engaged in conversation. Look to see if they are positive or negative, if what they offer contributes to unity or discord, and so on. Observe who becomes the center of the discussion. These are all clues that may point to a person interested in others—an essential quality of an effective leader.

5. Try out members as leaders of subgroups. If your group is large enough, you can subdivide it for portions of your meeting time. For example, divide into two groups of five to discuss some questions related to the Bible application. When you do this, ask a couple of group members to lead the two subgroups. This will give you a chance to observe them in leadership situations.

If you use the subgroup approach, it is important that you coach each subgroup facilitator. Give them the basics of leading a discussion, and be sure they have the study guide before the meeting. It is wise to visit together about problems and ask for praise reports after the CareRing concludes. In all of this you will be preparing the way for your people to take on the role of group leader.

Obstacles to Developing New Group Leaders

No matter what techniques group leaders may employ, there are few skills that matter more to the future of your small group ministry than the ability to find and develop new leaders. Many leaders fail in this area. Here are some common barriers to developing apprentices:

1. ***Fear of failure.*** Many pastors have failed to coach laymen and women in giving spiritual leadership and care. Consequently, we should not be surprised to discover that many laypeople are frightened when it comes to sharing their feelings, their dreams or even their failings with others. Their position in the fellowship has been based on authority, faithfulness, personality or business skill, not on their ability to feed and lead others spiritually. So naturally, when they look at the skills it takes to lead a small group, they are worried that they won't be able to do it adequately.

2. ***Busyness.*** Many people will attend a CareRing but resist the idea of leading one because it sounds like too much of a time commitment. They can't figure out how to build caregiving into their schedules. Life is running them instead of them running their lives. They have given in to so many time demands that they would be hard pressed to find a way to give even two to three hours in a week to leading.

3. ***Lack of vision.*** Often a group leader resists giving responsibility to another for fear he or she will no longer be needed. Sometimes leaders simply do not know what steps to take in getting a potential leader into the apprentice position. Sometimes they

don't have a strong enough commitment to the need for growth. Any of these views, even when held internally, will keep a leader from developing others. The leader lacks a sufficient vision for identifying and developing new leaders.

Each of these three obstacles can be overcome. People can overcome their fears by receiving training in leadership skills. They can open up space in their schedules for leading by getting control of their time. And leaders can recover a vision for developing apprentices by being convinced that their place will never be threatened and that, in fact, as they send others out to start new groups they may have an even greater sphere for service as a district coach. They are ready to move ahead in developing apprentices.

> *Leaders are developing skills, building knowledge of how to play the game and watching for personal readiness.*

Developing New Group Leaders

What is involved in developing apprentices? Allow me to begin by using some sports metaphors to get the ideas across. For one thing, the leaders see themselves primarily as district coaches in these ways: They "practice" with their leaders in training sessions. They evaluate how the plays were executed (people skills and use of group-building strategies). They play the game films back (reviewing step-by-step progress). They cheer on potential leaders from the sidelines (actually, from the other side of the living room), while apprentices are leading small parts of the CareRing. When the apprentices are ready, the player-coach knows they have effectively led every part of the CareRing week after week and have the confidence to take charge of their own group. Leaders are developing skills, building knowledge of how to play the game and watching for personal readiness. This readiness is the apprentice's desire and ability to lead others and coordinate all the activities of a CareRing.

More specifically, once a prospective leader is identified, the leader should do three things to initiate the growth process and move that person toward leadership:

1. ***Support the prospect with compliments where deserved.***
   This is not flattery. An example of flattery is making a general

comment about how well the evening went or how well the potential leader performed. Potential leaders typically read flattery as insincere, and therefore general comments like "You did a great job" are of little value. What these people need are compliments. So, what are compliments? They are specific observations voiced by the leader about the apprentice taking initiative, skillfully handling an objection, effectively intervening to resolve a conflict and so forth. A specific statement about the use of some skill or gift is a genuine compliment and is received as such by apprentices. This has value and therefore is encouraging to the apprentice.

2. ***Give small tasks to the apprentice.*** Early on, even before being approached about serving officially, the apprentice may be invited to make the announcements, offer an opening or closing prayer or perhaps lead an ice-breaker. As the prospect's confidence builds, the leader continues to compliment this person on his or her progress and give him or her larger tasks. Eventually, the apprentice will have led every part of the CareRing.

3. ***Approach the apprentice about taking leader training.*** The leader should take this step when he or she observes the apprentice responding, finding joy in leading and building rapport with members of the group. Then, when the apprentice agrees to move ahead and when the leader is relatively sure the apprentice will do a good job, the decision should be announced to the CareRing.

The announcement time can be especially positive if the apprentice shares his or her vision of leading, the sense that God has laid this ministry on his or her heart and solicits the prayers and support of the group. This helps them know that God is at work coordinating the steps toward a new group, and often this causes them to want to be part of starting the new group to support the apprentice.

Apprentices can take training any time between the announcement that he or she will be leading and the time he or she starts a group. The best time is as soon as possible. Training should be offered at least every two to three months so that new apprentices constantly have training available whenever they make the commitment to lead.

The Timing of New Leader Development

Remember that every person moves at his or her own rate. Most apprentices are ready to lead within a few months. Some prospective leaders, however, have had former experience leading small groups and are ready to lead within just a month or two. In any case, you should require training before apprentices begin actually leading their own groups.

There have been a few instances in my experience in which someone who appeared to be capable and ready actually was not. Even though I am always eager to find new leaders, I have found that patience and consistency pay off in the long run. So I place great value on excellence. One false start is counterproductive and may damage newer Christians.

There is a type of "creative tension" during this time as leaders monitor the process of development. On the one hand, it makes sense to be eager for leadership development. Once a new leader is in place, if training and coaching have been done well, a new CareRing will fill up within two months. Therefore, we often say that the only thing holding us back is not having enough leaders. We want to go ahead with finding and developing new leaders as fast as possible.

On the other hand, groups should not be rushed along too fast. This will reduce the bonding and give the impression that leaders are being "used" to build a small group empire. Furthermore, rushing new Christians into leadership may result in weak leadership or a false start, ending with the resignation of the new leader and the dissolving of a new CareRing. This can only do harm and be discouraging to other leaders.

> *Releasing an apprentice is a difficult step ... . Yet this is for the good of the kingdom.*

The balance here is for leaders to always look for potential leaders while not neglecting to shepherd group members between sessions. It means constantly working with people, openly giving leadership to them and consistently praying for new leaders. Work behind the scenes. Never make an open up-front announcement like, "We want to split up our group, so we're looking for new leaders." That is the one sure way to discourage anyone from stepping forward. The "creative tension" occurs between this more open public work with group members and the more private personal prayer and behind-the-scenes personal work.

Empowering New Group Leaders

Once an apprentice has completed training, has gained the necessary personal confidence and is ready to lead, one of the toughest things a leader faces is letting go of the apprentice. When a leader resists finally releasing an apprentice to his or her own group, we jokingly say that leader is having "prepartum blues." This condition is not experienced after the birth of a new group but before it.

Releasing an apprentice is a difficult step, one that some leaders have a tough time taking. Yet this is for the good of the kingdom. It is for the sake of the cause of Christ that we move ahead. We are not in this for ourselves.

Far too many capable leaders have crashed and burned because they wanted to build their own personal realm. For this reason, the small group pastor should have a personal interview with every trainee and actually quiz him or her on whether or not he or she understands the process of group reproduction. I ask my new leaders personally and privately if they will commit to the process of future group multiplication. This is not a point at which we can have lip service; only life service will do.

Empowering new leaders requires vision, commitment, skill and faithfulness. The care of others is dependent on this skill and the commitment to the concept. If we cannot enable trainees and then will not, or cannot, let them go, giving them the reins of leadership, then we, not they, become a lid on future growth.

Similarly, if potential leaders hedge about reproduction while being trained or do not quite comprehend it, it is often wise to put their leadership on hold and give them more time to catch on. Cue in their leaders to continue working with them and holding the value of reproducing themselves before them until the trainees catch the vision.

Also, empowering apprentices means leaders support them and their

> *Getting together causes them to see that they will not stop being friends and being part of each others' lives just because the new group has started.*

leadership before an existing group. Often, the potential leader will train an apprentice but will fail to state his or her confidence in the new leader and support the apprentice orally to the group. This can leave the members feeling that the apprentice is a helper or coleader. Only the leader can truly empower that trainee and build confidence in that person within the group. For there to be a smooth transition to a new group, the leader remains the key. If the leader is optimistic, if the leader keeps the vision and purpose before the CareRing and if the leader expresses confidence in the apprentice during this whole process, then formation of the new group will go well.

For both—the original group and new group—to continue to be healthy and productive they must avoid another danger. Earlier I talked about "prepartum blues." But after the new CareRing has started, we can fall prey to "postpartum blues." This is observed as a loss of heart for the group by the leader. When either the new leader or the one who stays with the original group allows himself or herself to be hurt, disappointed or otherwise discouraged because there are not as many people as there were before the new group was started, then both groups and leaders may be damaged.

One of the best ways to counteract "postpartum blues" is to make the "birth" a celebration. Have a party the last night both groups are together. This puts the focus on advancing kingdom work and reminds everyone that you have achieved one of your original missions.

Many original and new groups will even make it a point to get back together once a month after the new CareRing is started. This helps members of the original CareRing see that what they have done is valuable. Getting together causes them to see that they will not stop being friends and being part of each others' lives just because the new group has started. This is part of empowering the new leader.

NEW DISTRICT COACHES

For growth and reproduction to run smoothly, not only must new leaders be found to lead new groups but also new district coaches must be found to lead new huddles. Once a small group pastor has more than five or six groups in his or her church, he or she must create district huddles. This means gifted, experienced leaders must be found for the new huddles. As growth continues, more huddles and district coaches will be needed.

Think you can dispense with district huddles and district coaches? Not so. Lack of huddle organization is often a hidden killer of small group ministries. Not being organized to coach new leaders, not having time to work in excellence with groups or not developing huddle leadership can cause a ministry to grind to a halt. It is not an option, therefore, to be unorganized, to go about group leadership casually or to overlook leadership development. Raising up leaders who succeed in finding new leaders and in multiplying their groups must become a way of life. Those are often the people who become your new district coaches, each leading up to five groups.

> *The district coach is in a position of considerable influence over the small group ministry, so picking the right person is crucial.*

As with group leaders, the process is one of finding, developing and empowering your new district coaches.

Finding New District Coaches

Locating a new district coach is not always easy, but the rewards are immense. The district coach is in a position of considerable influence over the small group ministry, so picking the right person is crucial. Don't undertake it without much prayer and reflection. Take your time and make the right choice. That's better than having to deal with the problems that arise from a mistaken choice.

In many ways, the same processes discussed earlier regarding individual groups also apply at the huddle level. District coaches watch for effective leadership and are always giving their leaders experiences that help them lead the district huddles. The district coach is also always observing leaders for effectiveness and giving encouragement to them when they succeed.

Developing New District Coaches

Once again, the processes of observation, encouragement, coaching and empowerment apply to district coaches. The Serendipity leadership seminar will give leaders of leaders a comprehensive needs assessment of new leaders so they can train and serve potential leaders best. Yet there are some differences between the way group leaders and district coaches function.

So much hinges on whether or not we have strong, faithful district coaches that we must monitor this process carefully. It only takes one nonfunctioning district coach to harm or potentially destroy a huddle and many years of work former leaders have done. The best way to save headaches and heartaches is through training and careful observation of each potential district coach.

Once identified, an apprentice coach is placed with an experienced district coach for a few months to work alongside and learn from him or her. The actual amount of time spent in apprenticeship depends on the confidence level and the skill level of the potential district coach. Often two months is an adequate period for this apprenticing, though in our church we have taken up to a year for the total apprenticing process.

The following training device is useful in bringing up both new leaders and new district coaches. After each group (for the leaders) and each huddle (when raising up a district coach), ask the apprentice these questions:

- What went well?

- Where did you get stuck?

- What would you do differently next time?

The value of asking these questions is that we are not telling but asking. The genius of the questions is that the trainees are spotting the needs and setting their goals in response to them. By asking three simple questions, we are guiding the trainee to focus on specific needs he or she has in leading.

Empowering New District Coaches

Deploying new district coaches requires a process similar to developing new leaders. This time, however, they need to be bonded with other district

> *Another setting in which all district coaches should be involved is training.*

coaches. They also have to connect with the leaders who will work with them. Each district coach who is coaching a potential district coach will need to be sure every leader in his or her huddle sees the qualities of that potential district coach, and is helped to value his or her leadership.

The pastor, too, must give value to that person and his or her leadership. This can be done with other leaders and should include commissioning in a public worship service by the pastor and key leaders of the ministry. We include a commissioning service in our worship setting once a quarter. Some churches will do so a couple of times a year, depending on how often they offer training and how many new leaders they have.

As with all other district coaches, any apprentice becomes part of the leadership team. An apprentice should be involved in district coach retreats and the monthly training with the small group pastor, and should be considered a district coach from the beginning. It is important to put them in situations where they can learn from and get to know the other district coaches well. Even more so, you must empower them as huddle leaders. You are saying, "These people are now on the team."
Another setting in which all district coaches should be involved is training. I had been training new leaders for more than five years when I realized that I had been making a big mistake. We were saying that the district coaches were leaders, but I was the only one doing the teaching. I began using as many district coaches as possible to share the training, and the whole personality of leader training changed for the better. For the first time, every new leader got to know many of the district coaches. Also, the district coaches all realized they were an integral part of the training experience. This helped them gain experience and built their confidence to a new level. This was one more way in which the district coach was empowered.

A trained and empowered district coach, just like a trained and empowered group leader, is ready to minister fully within your small group ministry. As you watch how the Lord uses this person, you'll know the sense of reward that comes from being faithful in this other job of yours.

Chapter Eleven:
A Wagon Built on the Go: Materials for Constructing a More Complete Ministry

A farmer in the Old West, living miles from town, had only a team of horses and the wheels, frame and seat to an old buckboard. He could ride in it, but as it lacked boards, he could not load anything in it. One day the farmer needed to go to town for supplies. What could he do? He decided to start out with what he had, hoping to find boards along the way to town. He would then finish the wagon as he rode along, adding whatever boards he could find. Sure enough, by the time he got to town, he had finished the buckboard. He picked up his supplies and returned home. If he had never started out, he could not have made progress. He had to build his wagon as he went.

A true story? Probably not. But it makes a point that's true of our small group ministries. You don't need to have everything in place to begin. Don't feel that because you can't start with a lot of trained leaders and the organization that some other church has, you should not start. Just start with whomever and whatever you have. Try to find the best potential leaders as you begin and put in place the key activities, and God will give you the others along the way. Build your wagon as you ride.

In this chapter and the next—our final two chapters—we will discuss dozens of proven methods for building a small group ministry. In this chapter, we will concentrate on building the ministry as a whole, while in the last chapter, we will look at building the ministry's leadership. Here are approaches and concepts that will bring new people into your ministry, your Sunday school and your church.

SMALL GROUP EVENTS THROUGHOUT THE YEAR

Every quarter the small group pastor holds a leadership summit with all CareRing Shepherds, and every month he or she holds a meeting with just the district coaches. Also every month, each district coach holds a district huddle with all of the group leaders and others leaders in his or her district.[1] And, of course, every week each group leader holds a CareRing session. These regular meetings keep the schedule rather full. There should still be room for an occasional special event, either for everyone who is involved or just for the leadership.

> *A healthy CareRing ministry has occasional special events scheduled to get people excited about the ministry once again.*

Just as we all need holidays through the year because the weekends are not enough of a break on their own, so a healthy CareRing ministry has occasional special events scheduled to get people excited about the ministry once again. What follows is a menu of special events, some of which you may want to schedule for your CareRing ministry. They have all been successfully field-tested.

In addition to the special events listed below, there are always banquets at a restaurant, day trips the leadership might take together, a ski trip or camp-out for small group leaders or other events the ministry can sponsor for the local church. Once Sunday school and small groups are linked together in the CareRing system, the small groups could naturally sponsor a teacher appreciation event for the adult Sunday school department. Be creative!

Here is my recommendation: As your ministry expands, think the year through and be sure there is a balance of events for various levels of leadership.

- Be sure to sponsor some churchwide events.
- Have an event for everyone in leadership.
- Offer an event for your district coaches and apprentice coaches.

In this way, every part of the team feels important and valued.

Fall Roundup

Many churches gear up for a new ministry season in the fall. What better time to get everyone in your church together who is connected with, or interested in, your CareRing ministry?

A fall roundup is basically a party whose purpose is to attract attention to the CareRings and to create positive relations with people in the church for small groups in general. It is an all-church event sponsored and planned by the small group ministry team. It works best at an outdoor setting early in the fall. It can be built around a western theme or simply a harvest theme.

> *A fall roundup is basically a party whose purpose is to attract attention to the CareRings and to create positive relations with people in the church for small groups.*

The roundup can be held at a nearby camp or retreat center. Even a large farm will do, if there are facilities available for all the events. This event can feature skits, a barbecue dinner, a hay ride, games for the families, a bonfire for roasting marshmallows, even fireworks.

You can promote CareRings by giving a brief, fun invitation to join in the form of a skit. Introduce the leaders and district coaches. Hand out flyers detailing when and where every CareRing in your church meets.

Central Community Church uses a western theme for our fall roundup. People who sell tickets wear cowboy hats and scarves at a table set up in a visible place three Sundays before the event. We call it the Triple-C Ranch Roundup. (That's "Triple-C" for Central Community Church.) This event is one of the most exciting and productive things we do to emphasize groups. It is very popular because it is loads of fun and is a tremendous start for the new year.

Midyear Leaders' Retreat

If your church operates on a ministry season stretching from early fall to early summer, then by midwinter—the middle of your ministry season—the energy levels of your leaders may be dropping. Get your leaders pumped up again with a midyear retreat. Let me tell you how we've done this at our church (where it is the fastest-growing event in the whole ministry).

For us, the midyear leaders' retreat is designed to be a quality event at a hotel that is loaded with amenities. We begin with fun get-acquainted games, great singing and a speaker. Afterward, people are free to play Ping-Pong or shuffleboard, go swimming, eat a late dinner, play table games or just visit. They love it.

The schedule goes something like this: We have a combined morning session and then break into huddles till noon. In the afternoon we use lay leaders (mostly district coaches) to lead top quality seminars in two sessions. We close with a great sit-down banquet, some fun skits, the presentation of the leaders of the year and a challenging message from our pastor. Between 7:00 p.m. Friday and 7:00 p.m. Saturday, we have packed in loads of quality ideas, great fun and powerful inspirational testimonies of what God has been doing that year.

This year we will ask everyone to bring a prospective leader or two with them. Then we will announce group leader training within a couple of weeks, hoping to sign up the prospective leaders.

Christmas Party

Consider having a Christmas banquet for all your small group leaders. This could be built around the theme "Thank You for Giving to the Lord" and could use that song as the theme. You could also use Christmas choruses that have the idea of giving in them. You might give a specially wrapped gift to each leader and host.

An excellent feature might be testimonials of how lives have been changed when Jesus came into a person's life through his or her CareRing, much like the way he changed the world when he came at Christmas. You could make this a family event and include a visit from Santa Claus. This would be a powerful time to restate your purpose to reach the lost like Christ reached out to us when he came to earth.

> *Restate your purpose to reach the lost like Christ reached out to us when he came to earth.*

A variation on this theme is to have each huddle do its own Christmas party. When we have done this, the people have said it built a stronger sense of huddle identification. If there are other ministry-wide events throughout the year, having each huddle do its own party at Christmas might be the way to go.

Spring Celebration Banquet

The leaders who serve so faithfully in your CareRing ministry deserve recognition. One great way to do this is to invite them to a spring celebration banquet. This event is for everyone who is a CareRing Shepherd in any capacity or is even thinking about becoming one. It is a perfect time for the top leaders to express their appreciation, to share victories and hear praise reports, and just to have fun together. It is a powerful way to bring your total leadership team together, helping them to see that they are part of something great.

At one celebration banquet at Central Community Church, we focused on appreciating the hosts. For this event we used the theme of lighthouses. A giant banner at the front said, "Thank You for Making a Lighthouse of Your Home." We had a sit-down dinner, with the youth department doing the serving. We purchased attractive decorative lighthouses for every table as a centerpiece. Those were given to the hosts or host couples near the end of the evening as a way of saying "Thank you" for their hospitality through the year. In all, it was a wonderful evening and sparked an abundance of appreciation both for the hosts and from them. At another banquet we honored all new leaders that year—43 in all! It, too, was a great evening.

Visioning Day

While the spring celebration banquet is for every CareRing Shepherd and all group members, a visioning day is just for the coaches and their spouses. This is an enjoyable event, but it also has a serious purpose. It is a chance to refocus on what the CareRings ministry is all about. You could spend a couple of hours reflecting on the past year, leading into planning for the new year and refocusing on your purpose and vision for the future.

Where and when you hold the visioning day are entirely up to you. A good time to schedule this day may be in the summer, before your ministry gears up for its next

> *Visioning day ... is a chance to refocus on what the CareRings ministry is all about.*

season in the fall. If you're looking to keep costs down, you could hold it at your church. You could also use a church camp for this event. We've even used two evenings in the summer for this coach's visioning day ... two Thursdays or two Fridays. A meal was included to start each evening.

A nice idea, if you can afford it, is for the church to pay for rooms at a nice hotel on a Friday night. Ministry leaders could use the evening for a meal together and fun playing golf or swimming. The next day you could use one of the hotel's conference rooms for morning and afternoon sessions.

After your visioning day, you're ready for the fall roundup, and the cycle of annual events start all over again. Bring these major events into existence as the ministry grows. Be sure to have lots of fun and ensure that each event has a clearly stated purpose.

GROUP BUILDING STRATEGIES

It should be obvious to you by now that the smallest unit of the whole CareRing organization is the CareRing itself. Much can be said for the huddles, for the coaches, for major events and so on—they are all important. But the CareRings themselves are the core groups. Without spiritual and numerical growth in CareRings, all the rest of the organization doesn't exist.

For this reason, let's review some common strategies for building the group and keeping its mission before members. They are: keeping the vision for evangelism before people through use of the "open chair;" inviting all to participate by welcoming everyone's point of view; increasing contributions to discussion and prayer by breaking a group down into subgroups of four each; bringing people together in social events.

The Open Chair

Of all the strategies I'm going to mention, none is so commonly discussed as the "open chair." Small group leaders all across the country promote this idea. Yet, as I have sat in on scores of groups everywhere I have gone, I have been amazed by how few of them actually put this idea into practice. I guess it's easy to forget its value or lose sight of the purpose behind it. So I'll mention it once more.

In case the concept of the "open chair" is new to you, here's how it works. Simply put, each host puts out not only enough chairs for all the people who attend but also one extra. This chair remains open, in plain sight of everyone, throughout the session.

The open chair may serve three purposes. First, groups can use the chair to visualize Christ himself sitting there as they pray. I know of one person in our church, Carolee Harshfield, who had never prayed aloud until the group she was in made a point of imagining Jesus to be sitting there. That night was a breakthrough for her. Second, groups use the chair to comment about those of their group who are absent that night. The empty chair reminds them to pray for the missing members. Third, and most importantly, they use it to remind themselves that there are still many in the world who do not know Christ. The open chair symbolizes the lost who might be reached with the Gospel and brought into the group.

Small groups are not about us, the "found," but about the lost men and women whom God loves. There is no other concern we must work so hard to keep before ourselves. It is easy to get wrapped up in our needs and the needs of our families and forget the thousands all around us who need God. The empty chair is a visual reminder that we are not through touching and reaching lost people for Christ.

> *Small groups are not about us, the "found," but about the lost men and women whom God loves.*

It's remarkable how something as simple as an empty chair can be used for so much good. Here are a few examples of how the open chair can be introduced creatively by group leaders:

- Have every member write down the name of a person at their workplace who seems to be open to the Gospel and responsive to them personally. Then, in prayer, have group members say the name of that person, visualizing him or her sitting in the chair. To some, this may sound a bit mystical, but if you try it, you will simply be visualizing in faith how God may impact their lives. After all, faith is "the evidence of things not seen" (Heb. 11:1, KJV).

- Have group members sit quietly, thinking of those they know. They should wait for the Lord to impress upon them the name of a neighbor, friend or relative. God cares about everybody! When the Lord has done so, the individual should pray for that person, asking God for the opportunity to share the Gospel and invite him or her to the CareRing.

- Lead the group to tell about someone whom God has laid on their heart—even someone who is not in town. Have them share with the group who these people are and why they are concerned about them. As the CareRing members enter prayer time, challenge them to agree in prayer with each other for those seekers who have been mentioned.

- If your CareRing members have not brought names to the group in a few weeks, let the chair represent people you should care for and should be praying about. Ask God to lay a burden of concern for someone on the heart of each person present. Challenge your people to accept a person as a prayer and witnessing project. Then stand back. If you were sincere in offering yourselves to God, he will answer.

Leveling the "Playing Field"

Not everybody feels they can make a contribution to the CareRing. Some don't believe their opinions will be heard, much less appreciated. For them, a small group may be an intimidating environment. They may never come back if they didn't feel welcome and valued.

The group leader's role, in part, is to insure that everyone (especially new members) knows they are accepted and that what they say is important. Part of this process is to give the group experiences from the start in which they find they are all valued. One of the ways of doing this is to have them share information about themselves.

We are all experts on one subject—ourselves. We all know more about ourselves than anyone else does in the room. So when members introduce themselves to the group, follow up by having them tell their stories, share a concern or mention a value they hold dear. This levels the playing field.

Sounds simple enough, doesn't it? It is. But still, some leaders can't seem to catch on to this one. It totally eludes some people that a person might be intimidated by others who appear to know more about the Bible, about Christian life or about the church than they do. Yet that is exactly what happens any time a new group first meets.

We must take care to ask questions with multiple-choice answers so it becomes obvious very soon that there is not one "right" answer to be brought out by some more experienced Christian. We must express support for even the most obvious "mistake" in the answers given. This is not encouraging heresy or the dissemination of biblical misinformation; it is respecting each person's right to express a point of view.

Our task is to build relationships and encourage self-esteem. Invite and enable all of your group members to participate freely.

Fearless Foursomes

Occasionally, a leader will tell me how wonderful it is that his or her group has grown to 18 or 20 people. It is difficult for me to share his or her enthusiasm, knowing as I do that when a group gets above 12 members, the quality of discussion diminishes. As you've learned, I strongly urge all groups to make plans for multiplication even before they get to 12 members. But even if a group is of a smaller size, I will often suggest that a leader break his or her group into subgroups of four persons each for certain parts of the session. A subgroup like this is the least threatening size of group. We call this a "fearless foursome."

> When a group gets above 12 members, the quality of discussion diminishes.

There are at least two opportune times in a group session to break into these subgroups. The best time is during discussion of Bible application. A CareRing of 12 people can do three times as much when they break into three foursomes. Three people can be talking at any one time, and the amount and possibly the quality of discussion therefore increases threefold.

The second best time to use subgroups in a session is during prayer. As with discussion, using subgroups during prayer triples the number of people who can be praying at any one time. Three times as much prayer is not a bad thing! Nevertheless, you won't want to use subgroups in prayer every week, since having all pray together can build a stronger system of support for those in need and for those who are reaching out to others to bring them to God.

Please note that I don't recommend that subgroups be used for both Bible study and prayer time. There needs to be a significant amount of time for the CareRing to gather as a whole. If all a group does together is the ice-breaker and announcements, let's say, then they may not bond well. Still, a judicious use of "fearless foursomes" can help people feel more comfortable and open up more, thus indirectly helping to grow the group.

Social Events

> *The social strengths of CareRings are often the bait that brings people to them.*

Since small groups are built on relationships, it's not all study and no fun. In fact, the social strengths of CareRings are often the bait that brings people to them.

This goes back to the impersonal nature of the world in which we live. Most people today buy their gas with a card at the pump, get their money at an ATM machine, work at a computer, do their Christmas shopping on the Internet and watch actors live out fake lives on a TV or movie screen. Talk about impersonal lives! We know more about operating our cellular phones than about hearing the hurt in what another person is saying. We understand far more about pushing buttons than about connecting with people. These are the reasons having fun, learning to truly listen to others and sharing one another's hurts is so necessary.

> *We know more about operating our cellular phones than about hearing the hurt in what another person is saying.*

If, for example, your small groups do not meet in December and July, you have a couple months in which you can get together for social events. It is also valuable for each huddle to just have fun together. The leaders all need support, love, fun and social relationships as much as those who are in our groups. Here are a few fun things groups can do:

- meet for dinner together
- go bowling or golfing
- play a softball game in the summer and go on a picnic
- visit a rest home and then have pie and coffee afterward
- take a ski, hiking or camping trip
- do a mission project
- spend Saturday morning working at the church together
- plan a family day, taking all the families in the group to the zoo
- take your kids to a game park

The list is endless. Whatever you do, be sure there is fun and adventure in it.

The most important reason for these outings, events and meals is fellowship. More new people will come to a CareRing at a social event than a regular evening meeting. If your group attendance or spirit has leveled off, plan a special fun event and challenge members to bring someone from work, a neighboring family or a seeking relative.

> *More new people will come to a CareRing at a social event than a regular evening meeting.*

THE LIFE CYCLE OF A SMALL GROUP

Groups pass through four stages in their life cycle: birth, growth, development and rebirth. *Birth* is that exciting time when a new group is started. Before long, though, it passes through a stage of *growth* in which new members join and begin getting to know one another. Next, during *development,* the group achieves spiritual maturity and is working well together. Finally, as the group grows too large to be "small" anymore, it goes through a *rebirth* in which it divides, each half starting the life cycle all over again as an independent group.

To be healthy and productive, a group must keep moving through these stages. But sadly, not all groups do make it through all four.

Many CareRings, for example, have been birthed, have grown numerically and then have plateaued. Intimacy did not develop. Bonding was minimal. Such CareRings made it through the first two stages but never arrived at the third stage—development.

Then there are groups that have gone through all of the first three stages but never rebirthed. Possibly the leader did not take advantage of the bonding and intimacy that took place during the development stage. Result: instead of rebirthing, the group atrophied and died. He or she may not have held up the vision of growing and birthing a group. They might not have given leadership away, making room for potential new leaders.

> *A wise leader will urge his or her group forward at every stage of development.*

A wise leader will urge his or her group forward at every stage of development. CareRings are all about folding new people into the groups, caring for them and helping them to reach others. A group should never lose sight of its goal: growth and multiplication.

Before we take a closer look at the birthing process, let's look at how a group leader can move his or her group ahead.

Shifts in the Three-Part Agenda

Whether it's explicitly stated in a group or not, a CareRing normally has three parts to its "agenda," or the way it goes about its business. The three parts are ice-breaker (gathering), Bible application and prayer. Of course, it's up to each group, especially to the group's leader, to determine just how the agenda plays out.

> *Experience and time have proven that balance is essential to healthy groups.*

But one thing I've learned is that a wise leader can help his or her group move ahead by subtly shifting the emphasis among the three parts of the agenda.

But before I get to this strategy of agenda shifting, let me make it clear that I'm arguing for a shifting, not an imbalance. Experience and time have proven that balance is essential to healthy groups. For example, if the group overemphasizes Bible application, it becomes too studious and cerebral. When the agenda tips too heavily toward reflection, it turns others off because it appears to them to be too introspective and mystical. Still others may be alienated when too much focus is placed on interaction and caring and the group becomes more of a social club than a spiritual growth group.

Though each of the three elements is essential in itself, so is balance among all three. The wise leader will concentrate on including all three elements in the agenda. Also, a clear mission should permeate every element of a meeting. There must be a sense of purpose attached to all that the group does. At different stages of group life, this purpose might be either growth, spiritual maturity, evangelism or rebirth.

The three-part agenda elements will shift from time to time as the group matures. This creates the life cycle of the group. As a CareRing begins, there will normally be more emphasis on relationship building than on Bible study. Later, as the members bond with each other, the emphasis will shift to more concentration and time given to Bible application. Finally, as the CareRing moves toward rebirth, the amount of time and emphasis will shift to others. Yet throughout this process, all three parts of the agenda will be observable.

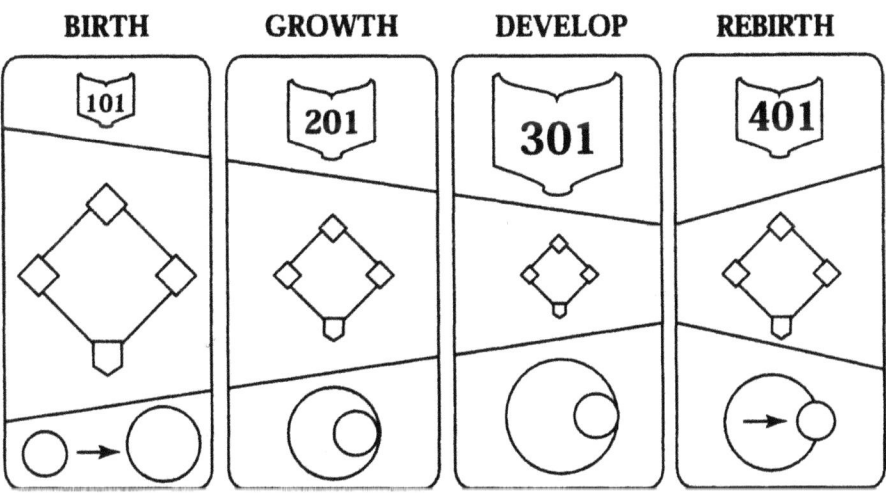

This process of slowly shifting emphasis on each of the three parts of the agenda does two things for a group: First, it keeps the group moving. Like anything else, groups can easily get bogged down. They can atrophy and slowly die for lack of exercise, nourishment and a challenge. Second, the process gives the leader a gauge by which he or she can evaluate the health of a group. Similarly, by watching the agenda

> *Like anything else, groups can easily get bogged down. They can atrophy and slowly die for lack of exercise.*

of a group over a few weeks, the leader can see where the CareRing is in the life cycle process. This gives the leader a diagnostic tool and enables him or her to move the group on toward the next step of maturity.

Mastering the ability to shift emphasis in the agenda gives the leader a powerful tool in moving a small group ahead.

Strategies for Birthing

As with all family plans, the leader and group must decide within their hearts that having a "child" is what they want to do. The three stages of the process might be summarized as family planning, the three trimesters and the birth. Let's follow these three parts of the rebirth process, followed by nursery care.

- **Family planning.** First, the parents decide they want a child. In group life, this means that the leader and apprentice must know in their hearts that this is what they want. This is important because God designed his family to grow (Matt. 13:1–23). It is important since we all reproduce ourselves in others. When we truly want to start another group, those around us will too (Matt. 10:24–25). And the best way to expand our ministry is by reproducing ourselves (2 Tim. 2:2).

There are some serious side effects when we don't reproduce. For one thing, not everyone will be able to share or participate as the group continues to grow. Some members will lose interest and attendance may drop off. Other members will start arriving late or leaving early, giving evidence that the group may not be a high priority.

On the other hand, as the leaders and group decide to grow and birth a new group, there are some positive advantages. Morale will be kept high as members see progress being made toward their mutual goal of birthing. More people will stay engaged with the group because more of them can feel they are an integral part of the group, its work, and its progress of moving toward the mission of birthing. The number of people involved in a group will grow, as will the number in the whole small group ministry.

Second, leaders must begin developing apprentices as early as possible. From the very beginning, if leaders hold up the vision of starting another group, other potential leaders in their CareRing will begin to believe they can be a part. The dream of growing, of their possible involvement and of birthing a group is exciting, especially to people with leadership potential.

- ***Three trimesters.*** In the "first trimester" leaders sow the dream up front. They share their heart about how exciting it will be to have a "baby" group born. They deal with the "morning sickness" of objections and fears in group members. There are a host of concerns CareRing members have when first hearing about this possibility:

Fear of change is one concern. At this stage, fears need to be identified and addressed.

Another concern is for relationships. Many members fear they will not be able to stay with their friends. Help them see that, with two groups, they will still be able to be with those they feel closest.

Another concern is lack of vision. Some simply don't understand why you're doing this. Talk about the vision and help them see how exciting this will be for God's work.

During the "second trimester" you might hear people saying, "This isn't so bad." They learn that you're not going to take the baby by cesarean section! Members discover that this is a process and see that you have their best interests at heart. Through this time the leader should build relationships with members, making phone calls to check on them and meeting with them one-on-one.

Most of all, the leader should concentrate on finding and developing the apprentice. It's best to have a couple of prospects for new leaders in mind. Years of experience have taught me that no other single task is more important than this. Begin giving small parts of the group agenda to those potential leaders. Evaluate their response and give them room to make mistakes. Most of all, help them build their self-confidence and teach them why you're doing what you do through this process. Help them see the purpose, vision and process. Chapter twelve has much more on this whole process.

The "third trimester" is climactic. Tension may develop during this period. The group may feel uneasy and members might be unable to articulate why they feel this way. During this time, leaders should concentrate on the emotions within the group. They should encourage openness and watch for warning signs, such as sporadic attendance, complaint, lengthy meetings or loss of energy within the group. The best remedy of these maladies is open and honest sharing. Here the leader keeps the purpose clearly before the CareRing.

Another important factor for leaders is that they make specific plans: They need to set a "due date" for the baby. They'll want to work especially closely with the apprentice and do lots of subgrouping. Then they'll need to decide who will be in each group (as we'll discuss in chapter twelve). Yet you shouldn't place anyone in a group without their input.

- *The birth.* Leaders will need to be on the alert for "complications" just before the birth. As with any birth, the "doctor" will need to be an active participant in the process and the true leader of each group. Remind everyone that Christ is truly the "Great Physician." We take our orders from him. Have buckets full of the hot water of a pure spirit and yards of clean motives on hand.

One caution: watch for troubled members and readily discuss honest reservations or even objections. If you don't deal with them here, they will certainly resurface later.

- *Nursery care.* Just like any newborn, baby groups can mess up a number of things: they can make a stink and not even know they did it. Phew! They can complicate your schedule with problems that keep you awake at night. They can even irritate you with their incessant crying for food. They may just need to be held and loved.

One thing is certain: baby groups are fun. They take time, attention and megawatts of energy, but when they start to grow, they're so cute! They make you want to hug them and hold their hands while they struggle to learn to walk. You can't even understand them at first. They may have the colic of selfishness and keep you up late at night. When you listen to them, that "burp" of complaining just needs to be expressed. Then they'll go on to be happy.

RESOURCES FOR LEARNING MORE ABOUT SMALL GROUPS

This book and its related materials give you everything you need to start a CareRing ministry in your church. The basics are all here. But there is always more to be learned about small groups. (That's one reason there is a bibliography at the back of this book. We want you to keep on reading!) If you're planning on starting a small group ministry, or if you've already got one in place (perhaps especially if you've already got one in place), get in touch with some other resources about small groups. Sometimes we can get so focused on our program that we forget there are other ways of doing things.

I've been involved in small group ministry for 14 years, yet I keep on learning new things. Local churches, parachurch organizations and publishers have plenty of information they are eager to share with others. I've discovered that the resources fall into two categories: (1) resources offered by local churches, and (2) resources offered by organizations.

Resources Offered by Local Churches

Many local churches have developed small group plans and programs that are inventive and creative enough to be a wonderful resource for you. It's always interesting to know what works elsewhere (although you should not, of course, presume that just because a plan worked in another church it will necessarily work in yours). Some of these churches hold conferences where you can learn what they are doing. Others would be glad to let you just drop in and see for yourself what's happening.

Willow Creek Community Church in South Barrington, Illinois is a large and influential church that holds regular leadership conferences. I have visited this church four times, and each time I have been there I have learned more than I could assimilate. A remarkable story, Willow Creek now has more people attending small groups each week than it has in worship.[2]

Saddleback Church in southern California is another church I have visited repeatedly. Though their approach to small groups is different from that at Willow Creek, they are truly making an impact unique among small group churches and appropriate to their subculture.

This "purpose-driven church" concentrates group ministry on the developmental levels of its people.[3]

Southeast Christian Church in Louisville, Kentucky is one of the most rapidly growing churches in America today. Southeast's ministry is less structured than those of many group ministries in churches their size. There are two small group training events each year at Southeast that you could attend.[4]

Other churches doing interesting things in the area of small groups include Skyline Church in Rancho San Diego, California; New Hope Community Church in Portland, Oregon; Flamingo Road Church in Fort Lauderdale, Florida; and my own church, Central Community Church in Wichita, Kansas.[5]

Resources Offered by Organizations

Some organizations are designed specifically to help churches implement small groups. Some are organizations that hold seminars (often connected with publishing houses), while others are small companies that provide consultants.

- ***Seminars.*** Seminars typically provide excellent training by experienced trainers who are leading effective small group ministries in local churches. Content tends to be such that it can be adapted and is more general in application and scope. The best value is either to sponsor a seminar at your own church or to send as large a group as possible to a seminar outside your church (thus lowering your registration fees).

Many local churches offer training that leaders from other small group ministries can attend. Most of the churches listed above offer such training. Central Community Church is thus far the only church in the nation that offers seminars specifically for CareRing training. There are typically four seminars per year. Attendees can go to Wichita on Friday, stay in the home of leaders in the ministry to ask questions and learn from them, attend the seminar all day Saturday and normally fly or drive out that evening to be back for church on Sunday. The cost is relatively low, and participants have the option of setting up additional time to visit with pastors, interns or lay leaders in this CareRing ministry.[6]

- **Consultants.** Consultants come from either of two sources. The first are pastors or staff members who lead effective ministries in their own church and have been trained in consulting with small group ministries. Second, there are many specialists who work for major small group publishers or who are seminar sponsors who consult for local congregations.

As you consider working with a consultant, there are some important factors that you should include in your planning:

1. Check out the prospective consultant to be sure he or she has had some training in consulting with small group churches. The minimum should be to have been through the Leadership Network Small Group Consultants Forum.

2. Be sure to set up an arrangement with a consultant to work with you for a minimum of six months. This is essential. This ministry is so significant and complex that a one- or two-time visit is not enough.

3. Be sure your consultant will make himself or herself available to you by phone and e-mail for at least six months. If you are committed to a solid start, you will normally need in-depth coaching, encouragement and resource input for that long.

Chapter Twelve:
The Never-Ending Adventure: Unlimited Growth Through Excellence in Leadership

Perhaps the one area of small group development most important to the success of the entire ministry is building faithful and capable leaders. They are the ones who make small groups work.

In chapter ten we examined how to spot and develop apprentices, how to identify and develop coaches and how to empower group leaders. While these how-to's provide the specifics, what we have not developed yet is a broader view. So we now turn to the management and developmental aspects of the ministry as a whole in the local church. Here we'll look at the group leader's path to leadership, the tasks of upper-level leaders (district coaches and district coaches' coordinators), and at the roles of leaders in multiplying CareRings and huddles.

As you read this chapter, keep one fact in mind: You should concentrate on developing new leaders, not on developing new groups. If you have leaders, CareRings *will* form. So make your number one priority to develop new leaders. God and normal CareRing growth will take care of the rest.

> *Keep one fact in mind: You should concentrate on developing new leaders, not on developing new groups.*

THE PATH TO LEADERSHIP

We've already discussed how group leaders are responsible for developing other leaders by identifying group members who seem to have leadership ability and then mentoring them through an apprenticeship period. But the church has a responsibility in preparing potential leaders as well. The church must put in place a process to train, qualify and send out these leaders to do their work.

The path to leadership is for both leaders and hosts. But because leaders have a greater impact on the people in the group, the focus in our discussion of this matter will be on leaders.[1]

Here, in a nutshell, is a proven four-step process you may want to follow: First, when a group member has agreed to become an apprentice, he or she is taken through a training process. Second, the apprentice is interviewed by the small group pastor. Third, the other members of the pastoral staff are asked to give their approval or disapproval. Fourth, the apprentice is commissioned as a leader. Only by successfully completing all four steps is an individual ready to take on the leadership of a CareRing.

Let's take a closer look at each step.

Step 1: The Training Session

The event that comes first as leaders are developed is training. This is an extended period of time in which you get together a few apprentice leaders and potential hosts to teach them such things as the vision for your CareRing ministry, the organization of the CareRing leadership and the principles you follow. The focus, of course, is on the responsibilities of leaders and hosts.

> *Training is a way to make sure that the potential leaders are on the same page with you about your ministry.*

Training is a way to make sure that the potential leaders are on the same page with you about your ministry. It is also a way to give them the tools and the confidence to get started within their own roles. The actual content of the training is something you'll want to develop to match your particular ministry.

But as you think about training, remember this word: *variety.* I've learned that variety is a key to both scheduling your training and the methods you use to present your material.

- ***The scheduling of the training.*** People's schedules do not all fit into one pattern, and therefore neither should your training schedule.

Shift work, children's schedules and a dozen other variables in the lives of your trainees can force you to offer different formats.

The most common approach is one full day of training from 8 a.m. until 4:30 p.m. on Saturday. The second most popular approach is to spread training across five or six Wednesday nights. The point is not to pick one schedule for your training but rather to decide on two or more schedules and give your apprentices the opportunity to pick the one that works best for them. If you want to be sure to get your apprentices through training, give them options about when to attend.

- ***The teaching styles used in the training.*** Early on, I taught almost exclusively with the lecture method. Over time, though, I began to see that lecturing alone was inadequate.

Research shows that people learn more and retain what they learn longer, when a wide variety of teaching methods are used. The worst teaching method is whichever one you use all the time. Spice up your teaching. Use a variety of methods. Provide a notebook. Play a video clip. Write on overheads. Have the participants fill in the blanks of preprinted sheets you provide. Break the group down for discussion. Take people through the actual experiences of such things as ice-breakers. Get other people, such as your district coaches, involved in teaching. And of course, use lots of humor and keep the energy level up.

> *The worst teaching method is whichever one you use all the time.*

Let me give you three reasons why you should use such varied teaching methods. First, everyone learns with a different style. Some are visual learners; others learn through oral instructions; most learn through experience. The methods used to teach should vary, so people with every learning style can understand and learn.

Second, everyone learns through repetition. So the more ways you can present an idea, the better. Each approach reinforces the other types of presentations. For example, showing a video clip from a movie and then having a discussion about it can be an excellent strategy. This stimulates participation, causes people to think and enables participants to discover key points for themselves. Making a point with an explanation, some participation and an observation repeats and strengthens the point, helping everyone remember it better.

Third, using variety in teaching methods will model more effective leadership for those being trained. If they were to hear you talking all the way through training, they might conclude that that's how they were expected to lead a group—by lecturing the group members the whole time. Never! There should be variety, fun and excitement in a CareRing session, so there should be variety, fun and excitement in the training of CareRing Shepherds, too.

• ***Introduction of leaders to ongoing training.*** Of course, the training of leaders is not complete after the initial session. Training is an ongoing process as well. You'll be training leaders monthly through the district huddle and the district coach meeting. Get your apprentices into these meetings as soon as they've been through the initial training, signed their covenant and received pastoral approval.

Step 2: The Interview by the Small Group Pastor

At the end of the initial training session, ask people to pray about the decision to become a leader. Walk them through what will be asked, show them the CareRing Shepherd-Leader and Host Covenant (see Appendix C), and challenge them to pray about whether or not God wants them to take on this ministry. At this point, some may choose not to lead. That's fine. It's better to learn up front that they are not really committed or suited to shepherding than to discover it after they take over leadership of a CareRing.

But for the apprentices who believe God is leading them to go on, ask them to call and set up a half-hour appointment with the small group pastor. During the interview, the pastor should try to get to know them better and get a sense of how well they understand the role of a group leader and how committed they are.

Here's a tip for the small group pastor. In the interview, ask the apprentice to repeat back to you what he or she remembers as the key points of the training. These ideas could include the following:
- Groups must maintain confidentiality.
- Leaders must not permit gossiping.
- Leaders must not permit discussion about politics or denominations.
- Leaders have two jobs: leading a group and reproducing themselves.
- A group session should have a balanced three-part agenda: caregiving, Bible application and prayer.

- No individual should dominate a discussion.
- A group should start and end on time.

Other points may be appropriate responses as well.

Pastor, when listening to the apprentice, think not only about how many of the ideas above he or she got, but also how many he or she did not get. That way, you can fill in the missing parts for him or her during this interview. This is another form of learning through reinforcement. Try to be sure no one goes away without a clear idea of the main points.

In that interview, you should also walk the apprentice through the CareRing Shepherd-Leader and Host Covenant point by point. Make it register with him or her that every one of the requirements in the covenant is important. Here are a few of the standards for leaders:

- They must have a personal relationship with Jesus Christ.
- They must be members of the church.
- They must regularly attend worship and Sunday school.
- They must be loyal to the church leaders.
- They must give regularly to the church from their financial means.
- They must be committed to living a moral life in every way.

These requirements may appear stern and even narrow, but there is a reason for that. If you ask much of people, they will live up to it; if you ask for little, they will live up to that, too. In short, you get what you ask for. Consequently, with high standards in place, being a CareRing group leader means something. It includes a commitment to a quality lifestyle and it stands for integrity. You will, of course, want the standards you set to fit your theology and understanding of biblical teaching.

> *If you ask much of people, they will live up to it; if you ask for little, they will live up to that, too.*

At the end of the interview, ask potential leaders to sign the covenant if they agree with it. This makes the commitment serious and official. And if there is ever a question about what your church means by living a distinctive Christian lifestyle, you can refer to the covenant.

> *Once people have seen what is expected of them, many have made new and deeper commitments to God.*

Seldom have I had a potential leader who was unwilling to sign the covenant. Actually, the opposite has more often been true. Once people have seen what is expected of them, many have made new and deeper commitments to God. I have had some, at this point in the proceedings, pray for forgiveness for some wrong they have committed. It was a new day for them. They could now lead with confidence and a clear conscience.

Step 3: Approval by the Pastoral Staff

Once potential group leaders are qualified through training and a successful interview with the small group pastor, ask the pastors of the church to verify them. If you want, each pastor could interview each leader. But it's not necessary to go that far. The small group pastor just needs to contact other pastors, if there is more than one, tell them who is up for leading new CareRings, and ask them if they have any comments or objections they want to share.

Sometimes other members of the pastoral staff may know something about the candidate that raises a red flag. A pastor may know about a conflict, poor people skills, unchristian behavior or something else that could disqualify the candidate. Better to know this ahead of time and resolve it in an appropriate manner, than to have the issue come up as a surprise after the leader has begun leading a group. Asking other pastors to review the histories of candidates in the CareRing ministry also helps to bind them together as a team.

It may appear as though this step applies only in larger churches, but I recommend you follow it even if your church has only two pastors. It can be that useful to you.

Step 4: Commissioning and Celebration

When an individual has been accepted as a new CareRing Shepherd, it's a big deal for him or her—and for your church! It's entirely appropriate to recognize this milestone in a public way. I recommend two kinds of recognition: (1) a commissioning service held as part of a worship service, and (2) a celebration at the next district huddle.

- *The commissioning service.* Plan to commission every group leader in a Sunday morning worship service. Here is how the commissioning service might go:

First, ask all new leaders to come forward. As they do, the small group pastor can introduce what is happening and read an appropriate Scripture, perhaps Acts 20:20 or 20:28.

Next, have the new leaders repeat aloud a "Shepherd's Commitment." It might run something like this: *"Recognizing my responsibility to make disciples, and in full dependence on Christ the 'Good Shepherd,' I covenant with God to pray faithfully for those in my care, to apply the principles of God's Word to my life and to lead someone into the fold this year. By the grace of God, I shall so live."*

Then all other leaders, hosts and district coaches can be invited to gather around, placing their hands on the shoulders of the new leaders. The pastor can lead in a prayer of commissioning for the new leaders.

Finally, you can present each new leader with a certificate stating the purpose for the occasion, the date and their name. This will serve as a memento of the special day.

This all might seem like a lot of trouble to go to. But it is important to honor new leaders publicly for at least three reasons:

- **First, it ensures that the position of leader is valued.** You need the people of your congregation to know it means something for a person or couple to serve in this way. This position is vital to the health and growth of the fellowship.

- **Second, a commissioning service lets your entire congregation know who the leaders are.** People need to know who to turn to when in need. When anybody wants to become part of a CareRing, you'll want them to recognize the names or faces of the leaders so they know who to go to.

- **Third, the service tells the leaders themselves that their position truly matters.** In the spirit of 2 Timothy 2:2, you are placing others into the hands of these leaders, entrusting them with the spiritual well being of your people. This is serious business. Let every new leader catch that seriousness

> *Let every new leader ... realize how vitally important it is that they live above reproach and take this ministry as a divine obligation and trust.*

and realize how vitally important it is that they live above reproach and take this ministry as a divine obligation and trust.

- *The district huddle celebration.* A district huddle is a more intimate environment in which to recognize the new leaders in a less solemn way. The first time new leaders attend a district huddle, make a party out of it. Introduce the new leaders to the others who are attending. Lead in a round of applause for them. Have some special refreshments in honor of them.

Making the first district huddle a party is a sure way to make new leaders feel welcome to the leadership structure of which they are now a part.

A CLOSER LOOK AT UPPER-LEVEL LEADERSHIP

Along with the small group pastor, the district coaches bear the greatest responsibility for training and developing the leadership of the CareRing ministry. We will take a closer look at what district coaches do, on an ongoing basis, to build up the CareRing leadership team. We will also take a look at those who supervise the district coaches in larger churches: the district coaches' coordinators.

The District Coaches' Tasks

District coaches deserve our respect. These faithful volunteer workers have a heavy burden of responsibility on them, and a significant amount of their spare time goes toward helping others.

District coaches have four operational tasks before them:

- attend district coach meetings
- lead the district huddle
- meet individually with leaders in their huddle
- visit CareRings in their huddle

These are the basics of their work. These four settings also provide a variety of opportunities in which the district coach can work with, love, pray for and serve the leaders and the new apprentices.

I recommend that you ask every district coach to do a minimum of one supervisory task a week. Here's how that can work: One week a month, a district coach attends a meeting with all other district coaches. A second week, he or she visits one of the CareRings in their district huddle. A third week, the district coach meets with a leader one-on-one. A fourth week, he or she leads the district huddle. These tasks may be done in any week of the month; there is no particular order. Only the week for the district coach meeting is set by the church.

The district coach also has one ongoing task: to identify and develop apprentice coaches. We'll take a look at that task a bit later. First we'll take a look at the three monthly operational tasks for which district coaches have major responsibility.

- **Leading district huddles.** A primary component of the district coach role is leading monthly meetings with all the leaders under him or her that we call district huddles. Huddles may be held in a home, at a restaurant, at an office or at the church. They are informal and never last more than two hours. Most coaches design their huddle around a meal or at least have someone bring refreshments. This setting gives each district coach the opportunity to grow in leadership themselves and build strong leaders of the leaders they serve.

The huddle involves three elements. The first is community building. Each district coach is taught to make his or her huddle a type of CareRing for those leaders. District coaches should try to give leaders a safe environment in which to share frustrations and talk openly about any problems or needs within their groups. They should strive to feed them spiritually and challenge them toward personal growth.

> *Each district coach is taught to make his or her huddle a type of CareRing for those leaders.*

The second element of a district huddle is ongoing training of group leaders and other leaders. There should be something in every huddle for each host, apprentice and leader. The district coach should work to continuously move his or her group of leaders, hosts and apprentices on toward being stronger leaders and more deeply committed servants.

The huddle's third element is comprised of various "housekeeping" tasks. For example, in our church a different huddle schedules people to man a small group information table in our church foyer each month. So at the huddle, a district coach who knows it's his or her huddle's turn to do this job can ask for volunteers.

• **Conducting "one-on-ones."** As the name suggests, a "one-on-one" is a face-to-face meeting attended only by the district coach and one of the leaders in the huddle. Each district coach should meet individually with each leader once every three or four months. Of course, a district coach should never meet alone with a group leader of the opposite sex. When a couple are leading a group together, the "one-on-one" is really a "one-on-two."

Many needs can be communicated in a huddle, but only in the one-on-one can the district coach really hear each leader and respond to the leader's needs. In these get-togethers, it's especially important for district coaches to listen for "hidden" needs as well as those needs openly discussed by the leaders.

The district coach wants to build strong relationships with leaders in these meetings. Also, this is the best place for a district coach to deal with any weaknesses leaders may have. (It's never a good idea to correct a leader in front of the other leaders.) The district coach should pray with their leaders. He or she may also need to offer words of encouragement.

• **Making CareRing visits.** Every month the district coach should make a visit to one of the CareRings in his or her huddle. If a huddle has four CareRings, for example, this means every group has a visit from its district coach once every four months.

This visitation does at least three things. First, it helps the district coach stay in touch with the situation each leader has to work with. Some problems may seem overblown to the district coach when he or she hears about them from a leader. But when he or she makes an on-site visit, suddenly the district coach realizes the leader wasn't exaggerating.

A second benefit of a visit to a group by the district coach is that it lets the leader know that his or her district coach is standing behind him or her to back him or her up. So, during a visit, district coaches often make some statement about what a great job the leader or host is doing. The district coach looks for ways to be supportive.

Third, the presence of the district coach says to each member, "You are being cared for. You're not just doing your own thing; you're part of something much greater than yourselves." This will help the group members catch the vision for what the CareRing ministry is about.

• ***Developing apprentice coaches.*** Though not one of the four weekly tasks of the district coach, developing an apprentice coach is a vital part of the ongoing growth strategy. Just as the only way new CareRings develop depends on new leaders, so the only way new huddles are born is with new huddle leaders.

Every apprentice coach is challenged to look for the leader that has been effective over a period of time. They are urged to use that person or couple to help lead the huddle. As these potential apprentice coaches build confidence, they are asked to pray about becoming a district coach. When the Lord leads someone in that direction, they are taken through district coach training and, when the huddle gets to six groups, they multiply and each one of them—the district coach and the apprentice coach—takes one of the new huddles.

As new huddles develop, they stay within the adult education class. Now the class has two huddles. Each of them functions within itself exactly as it did before multiplying.

The Role of the District Coaches' Coordinator

So far, this book has not said much about the district coaches' coordinator. That's because most churches don't have a large enough CareRing ministry to need this "district coach of coaches." But for those who do, the district coaches' coordinators are important people.

• **When a district coaches' coordinator is needed.** The position of district coaches' coordinator may be used in only about five percent of all churches. One reason is that there are not many classes large enough to need more than one huddle. Each huddle has up to five CareRings, and there are about 15 people who belong to each group (this is the number of people who will belong to a group, resulting in an average weekly attendance of about 12). With five groups per district huddle having 15 members each, there are 75 people ministered to in any one huddle. Not a lot of classes are larger than that.

However, when classes do grow significantly larger, it is easy for huddles to multiply. Then each class can have up to three huddles (or a total of 225 involved), thus accommodating unlimited growth. Then any class growing to this size would have a coordinator to work with each of the three district coaches. That person or couple would be the district coaches' coordinator.

Actually, though this might seem like an extreme case, we have two such classes in our church. Both of these classes have a district coach who led their huddle to develop six CareRings. The district coach found an apprentice coach to train, and they multiplied huddles. Their next step will be to go to a third huddle when each of the new huddles reaches six CareRings.

While this sounds a bit detailed, this explanation is intended to illustrate the capacity the CareRing method has to minister to unlimited numbers of peoples and in classes of all sizes.

• *What district coaches' coordinators do.* What are the expectations and people skills to look for in potential district coaches' coordinators?

Look for the same qualities at this level as you did when searching for district coaches. You are hoping to find people with motivational skills, men and women who know how to inspire and challenge other leaders and couples or individuals who have grown in administration skills.

Ask them to share in training others. Hopefully, they will become experts in finding and developing district coaches. Request that they be devoted to just the task of leading and feeding their district coaches and other leaders. Normally they will lead a couple of class-wide small group events each year to remind everyone that they are all part of a larger ministry that includes everyone in the class.

MULTIPLICATION MODELS

There are two secrets to building groups and a small group ministry. After prayer, hard work, loads of vision casting and training, the first secret to building groups is developing new leadership. The second secret is to start new

> *The first secret to building groups is developing new leadership. The second secret is to start new CareRings.*

CareRings. As mentioned earlier, when we concentrate on finding, developing and empowering new leaders, the new groups naturally follow.

Let's look at both what it takes to multiply CareRings and what it takes to multiply district huddles. There is a compelling vision in all of this that will motivate people and keep them focused. Life in general, and human nature specifically, being what they are, will pull us inexorably into a maintenance mode of leading small groups. The dream must be kept before our people, especially during the first years of a new small group ministry. This concern for multiplication and growth begins with the senior pastor and key leaders, but it must be an active concern in the minds of all leaders.

CareRing Multiplication

New groups grow faster than old groups. Two groups grow faster than one group. Small groups grow faster than large groups. For these reasons, we need to constantly start new groups.

While CareRing multiplication was discussed earlier, there are a few elements we have not covered. It bears repeating that birthing a group must be a vision given to every new group as it starts. CareRing Shepherds must lead their members to see how important this is. Reaching new people is what will keep us alive! Through a concern for reaching others, a profound sense of purpose will inspire and motivate all our people.

Along with this is the prayer for and commitment to new prospective leaders. Each leader needs to be reminded of how important new leadership is. This commitment to find and develop apprentices also keeps leaders from becoming possessive of their CareRing. We want all our leaders to keep focused on our mission as a group.

There are four common methods or ways to birth new groups. There does not seem to be any single best model. In fact, there is no wrong way to start a new group, assuming you are ethical and do not manipulate or coerce people in any way. There are probably more ways to start new groups, but here are four of the most common models:

• ***Model A: The leader takes the new group.*** In the first model, a leader raises up an apprentice. That apprentice takes over the existing CareRing, and the leader leaves to start a new group. Often a few members from the original group will leave with the leader to serve as a core of the new group.

This model looks like this:

L = Leader
A = Apprentice
NL = New Leader

        A L   ⟶   NL

    Original CareRing   **"Baby" CareRing**

This model typically works best in a healthy group where bonding has occurred between the apprentice and the group. Be aware that too many members may leave the original group and go with the leader. This happened just this year in the church where I serve. Fortunately, the apprentice couple was not so shaken by it that they quit. But it was discouraging and frustrating to them. When such a thing happens, it is crucial for the district coach and the small group pastor to give the new leaders their strong support. Better yet, the departing leader should urge members of the old group to stay in that group with the apprentice.

- *Model B: The apprentice takes the new group.* In this case the leader stays with the original group and the apprentice goes with a few members of the original group to start his or her own new CareRing. The original group carries on pretty much as it has, and the leader begins looking for a new apprentice.

Here's how this model looks:

        L A   ⟶   NL

    Original CareRing   **"Baby" CareRing**

This approach is especially effective when there is a strong apprentice or apprentice couple. On the other hand, if the original CareRing has gotten into a rut and has not grown much, perhaps it would give them a challenge if this was not the model used. They may be challenged more and caused to pay attention more if the leader left.

Of course, this decision has to be made by the leader, the apprentice and the district coach working together.

• ***Model C: The leader and apprentice each take a group.*** In this model, the group is essentially disbanded and its members individually choose which of two new groups—one led by the original leader, the other led by the apprentice (new leader)—they believe God is calling them to participate in. This is one of the most spiritually-oriented approaches to multiplying groups. Here's how it works.

A few months before the group leaders decide they are going to multiply, they ask members of the CareRing to begin praying for the Lord's leadership as to which group they should help. Week after week, the leaders share their vision of what God wants their groups to be. They may approach potential new apprentices for each new group during this time. It is also essential that during these weeks leaders constantly pray for new people. It is extremely important as well that they keep this purpose before their CareRing, reminding members of why we are doing this. They need to share from their heart the dream God has given them of reaching out and touching new men and women.

Then, on a specified date, they all meet and write either the name of the leader or the name of the apprentice (now the new leader), along with their own name, on a piece of paper. The papers are put in the middle of the circle, then opened and sorted.

Those people become the members of the new groups like this:

The leader and apprentice then finish the evening by praying with their new CareRing members and talking about the new direction in which God is leading them. This should be a time of celebration, focusing on the new people they will now be able to reach as two CareRings.

		L	A		
NL	←	or	or	→	**NL**
		A	L		

"Baby" CareRing   **"Baby" CareRing**

• ***Model D: The leader, the apprentice and a third person lead.*** This final multiplication model is for CareRings that grow rapidly.

Instead of dividing in two, the group divides in three. (Most CareRings birth one group; this birth is twins!) The leaders of the three groups are the original leader and either two apprentices or one apprentice and another leader brought in from the "outside" (probably a newly graduated apprentice from some other group).

This is what having twins looks like:

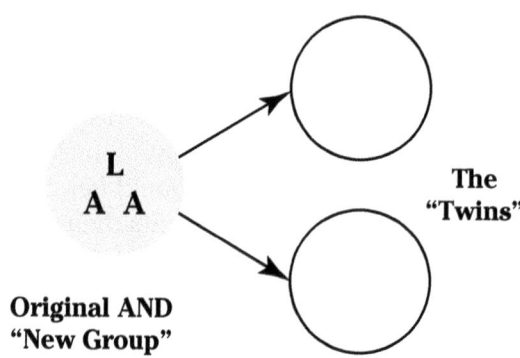

Original AND "New Group"

The "Twins"

(The shaded area is intended to show that part of the original CareRing goes with each new group.)

This model is not often needed, but there are times when it's the best choice. Many groups grow extremely fast. I have seen this among singles groups, in CareRings with unusually charismatic leaders and in a few groups with an unusually enthusiastic membership. These groups need to divide three ways if they are going to accommodate all their people and keep on growing.

I recommend that, in such a group, the leader regularly divide the group into subgroups for parts of the sessions and give potential apprentices charge of subgroups. In this way the leader will not only be seeing that the members of this large group get proper attention but will also be able to train a couple of apprentices at the same time. Thus the ground is being laid for the three-way division—an exciting event when it happens!

Huddle Multiplication

The multiplication of district huddles operates pretty much the same way as the multiplication of groups. Choose from among the models above and substitute "huddle" for "CareRing," substitute "district coach" for "leader" and substitute "district coach apprentice" for "leader apprentice."

One difference is that the leader who is being raised to the position of district coach must begin as soon as possible making connections with members of the other groups that will be in his or her huddle. These other group members may not know him or her well, and if he or she can quickly create rapport, it will help them feel more comfortable with the upcoming huddle multiplication.

> *Nothing can break the momentum and cause confusion more than leaders who don't function as a team.*

Another important thing to remember, as a huddle gets ready to multiply, is that the leaders need to keep in close communication with one another. Nothing can break the momentum and cause confusion more than leaders who don't function as a team. They need to stay in touch with each other weekly to discuss which members should go with which leaders and to keep each other abreast of developments and the feelings of members.

If you've reached the point of huddle multiplication, my advice is to take a moment and thank the Lord for how far you've come. You've taken that crucial step of deciding to integrate small groups with your adult Sunday school. You planned this new ministry. You made changes to your church's schedule to accommodate the new groups. You identified and trained the original leaders. These original leaders have gone on to reproduce themselves in other leaders. You have put a huddle organization in place. And now you're seeing that the CareRing approach can enable you to have unlimited growth in both your adult education program and your small groups. In short, you've done all that this book advocates. The Lord is blessing your church and using your CareRing ministry to serve many people. Give him thanks—then continue the adventure side by side!

Appendix A:
Questions & Answers

Q Is there a limit to how large a church can get with small groups?

A Possibly. Paul Yonggi Cho's church in Seoul, South Korea has grown to over 450,000 with small groups. In America, though, the largest church with small groups has about 18,000 in regular attendance.

Q Does everyone in the church need to belong to a CareRing?

A No more than all must sing in the choir or attend the Wednesday evening service. Of course, the broader the participation, the better. But starting with even two or three groups is a wonderful beginning for most churches.

Q What is the best time for CareRings to meet during the week?

A There really isn't a "best time." Rather, the "best time" is whatever works best for an individual group. Any day of the week can work, as can morning, afternoon or evening. Many churches, having found small groups to be a more effective ministry than the Wednesday evening or Sunday evening service, have eliminated that service and hold groups at that time instead.

Q What things are easily overlooked in forming and building small groups?

A Perhaps the easiest thing to overlook is the need to develop new leaders within existing groups. Growth will be held back if you can't identify, train and develop new leaders on an ongoing—indeed, an expanding—basis.

Another item often overlooked is the need to communicate some things right from the start. These include the evangelistic nature of groups, the requirement for confidentiality (we never tell something shared within our group), and the agreement not to discuss denominations, doctrine or politics.

***Q* What is the first thing to do before starting a ministry?**

A In a word, pray! Pray for clear directions and for God's guidance for you and others. Pray with anyone to whom he leads you. Share the need and let God burn a vision into your heart. When he does, you'll start with conviction and you'll be able to tell others what God has been doing in your heart.

***Q* How do we keep group leaders and apprentices enthused?**

A The best way I've found is through having them share stories with each other of victories in their CareRings. This mutual encouragement works best if you can find a time each month for all group leaders to meet. If that is not possible, then every other month is good, preferably at a time corresponding to a regular service (or even during the midweek service, if your pastor is agreeable). There is nothing quite like having someone come to these meetings down and tired and seeing that person leave with his or her head up and laughter in his or her voice. Having heard wonderful stories of what God is doing, that person realizes again that he or she is not alone.

***Q* How long should an apprentice serve before becoming a group leader?**

A This varies a lot from person to person. Some are ready in a matter of weeks; others take six to eight months before they feel confident. God will lead you, and them, at this point. Just be sure that as soon as they agree to start working toward serving as a group leader, you get them right into training.

Q What are some good resources on small groups?

A At the end of this book there is a bibliography with resources on everything from youth groups to Bible study methodology.

Q What other resources are available to help us get started?

A Companies like Serendipity and NavPress have excellent resources. I have become involved with a number of conferences and districts as a consultant. A group of churches will come together on a given weekend for a Friday night banquet and day of training on Saturday.

Individual churches have sponsored a similar weekend as a kickoff for the program. This works especially well for them because the initial event can also be set up to include consultation by mail or phone for six months following such an event.

Q Are there times of the year when you don't meet?

A Yes. Typically, we do not meet during December or July. In your area, it might be best to dismiss during both July and August. We have found that when we intentionally dismiss, people want to get started again in the fall or in January. Also, very seldom do groups stay strong during the summer, even though members may say they want to and may promise to attend. It's best to admit that we'll take a "vacation" and return in the fall.

Appendix B:
Core Values and Purposes of CareRings

As you plan your CareRing ministry, you may find it useful to establish the core values and purposes you see for the ministry. Here is an example of what you might come up with:

Core Values

- *Spiritual maturity:* Leading people to grow and become fully devoted followers of Christ.

- *Community:* Building community in which people know and feel that they belong.

- *Leadership:* Being a fully devoted disciple implies that a person be involved in leading others, holding them accountable, guiding them and assisting them to apply the Word of God to their lives.

- *Reproducing ourselves in others:* By definition, a mature Christian will be investing himself or herself in other believers by encouraging, training and empowering them to assume leadership.

Primary Purposes

- *Spiritual maturity:* A non-negotiable purpose of small groups is that we enable people to continually grow and become stronger in their faith and obedience. This embodies stewardship, worship, witnessing and so on.

- *Community:* While community is not the focus of groups, it is a product of them. Groups provide the only setting in the church where people come together to listen to and regularly support one another.

- *Spiritual leadership:* Small groups develop mature spiritual leaders who model authentic Christianity up close and personally for the people in their care. Unlike those occupying any other role in the body of believers, leaders are trained, monitored and guided regularly to lead others spiritually in order that they may grow in grace and knowledge of Jesus.

- *Reproducing ourselves in others:* Groups are committed to finding potential spiritual leaders. This includes a process of giving everyone opportunities to lead in prayer, of emphasizing Bible application and of having community-building experiences. Then they are observed, encouraged and invited to training where they are equipped to assume leadership. Finally, they serve as "apprentice leaders," receiving more guidance. As they assume the role of group leader, they have become a spiritual Shepherd. The leader has "reproduced" himself in another.

Secondary Purposes

- *Communication:* Small groups provide a communication system through which church leadership can present an urgent prayer need, emphasize a major event or even get an important in-house concern to the bulk of the congregation without ever making an announcement.

- *Keeping spiritual development central:* Groups bring people every week into the Word, call them to be accountable and offer prayer and support to one another. No matter how busy they get in doing church work, those in groups have a regular reminder that Christian life is about being people of God and his Word.

- *Belonging:* It is a proven fact that if people do not know someone personally at a church, they do not feel that they belong. Groups give every member a way to relate to others personally each week. In this way they know they are a part and feel that this is their church.

- *Informal support and counseling:* There is no way of knowing how many minor personal problems and concerns never grow into major problems (sometimes requiring intensive pastoral counseling) because there is weekly prayer in groups, someone to listen and mutual support from group members.

Appendix C:
CareRings Shepherd and Host Covenant

Since an overseer is entrusted with God's work, he must be blameless— not overbearing, not quick-tempered, not given to drunkenness, not violent, not pursuing dishonest gain. Rather he must be hospitable, one who loves what is good, who is self-controlled, upright, holy and disciplined. He must hold firmly to the trustworthy message as it has been taught, so that he can encourage others by sound doctrine and refute those who oppose it. (Titus 1:7-9)

I, ... (fill in your name), testify that Jesus Christ is my personal Savior and Lord and that I am a member of .... Church. Since I plan to serve as a .... (fill in role: group leader, apprentice leader or host/hostess), I commit myself to pursuing the qualities of an "overseer" found in Titus 1:7–9. I also commit myself to the following:

1. I will regularly attend worship and Sunday school.
2. I will faithfully give to the church.
3. I will attend training for my role in the CareRing ministry.
4. I will follow the leadership of my district coach and the church leaders.
5. I will seek to be a successful disciple maker.
6. I will seek the success of the church and its mission as given by Jesus Christ in Matthew 28:18–20.
7. I will live an exemplary life ethically and morally, including abstaining from chemical dependencies.

....
Name   Date

Appendix D:
District Coach Position Description

The District Coach is a leader and motivator of the Shepherd-Leaders of the small groups called CareRings. They provide pastoral care, support, encouragement and resources to the Shepherds under their care. They strive to live exemplary lives in faith, conduct and lifestyle.

- The District Coach supports and encourages all leaders under his or her care.

- The District coach leads a monthly gathering of all leaders in the district huddle. The purposes of the huddles is to minister to the Shepherd-Leaders spiritually, to give them resources and tools to help them grow as leaders, and keep a vision before them of the values and significance of the CareRing ministry.

- The District Coach is asked and expected to visit once a month with a Shepherd or Shepherd Couple. The purpose of this visit is personal coaching, prayer and encouragement to them as leaders.

- The District Coach monitors the CareRings in his or her care to challenge and help them develop new leaders. This includes assisting every Shepherd to have an apprentice, learning how to spot potential leaders and what to do to bring them toward leadership and help them mature, building confidence.

- They may be asked to share the training responsibility for new leaders.

- The District Coach is asked to visit one CareRing in his or her district a month making observations, helping Shepherds stay on track and coaching them personally one-on-one.

- The District Coach should plan to be faithful at monthly District Coach gatherings with the pastor, small group leader or staff member who leads the CareRing ministry.

Appendix E:
District Coaches' Coordinator Position Description

The district coaches' coordinator facilitates the ministries and activities of a group of huddles. He or she is a leader among leaders, a District Coach to coaches and a shepherd to coaches. The primary tasks of the district coaches' coordinator are encouragement, communication and team building. Skills necessary to be effective in this position include coaching, motivating, wisdom and a wide variety of people skills:

Primary Tasks

1. The district coaches' coordinator will coordinate the overall work and ministries of all the district huddles under his or her care. This involves careful communication (both with the small group pastor and with all district coaches on his or her team), vision casting and development of a cohesive team of district coaches.

2. The district coaches' coordinator's primary focus will be on the district coaches with whom he or she serves. They should strive to support, pray for, back up and lead the district coaches' team.

3. The coordinator should plan and lead gatherings with his team members at least quarterly. The role is primarily one of facilitating two or more huddles within a ministry area, such as singles, senior adults or young couples.

4. He or she should submit a quarterly report to the small group pastor and meet quarterly with the pastor for further coaching and development.

5. The district coaches' coordinator is responsible to the small group pastor and responsible for each of his or her district coaches. Whenever they can deal with a question of procedure, policy or other practices, they should do so. Otherwise, they should work with the small group pastor.

The Means of Ministry

1. The district coaches' coordinator helps keep each district coach on track with leadership skills, reporting and tracking of potential leaders in the groups of their district huddles. In other words, they help keep the ministry vision and objectives clearly before the leaders in his or her charge.

2. He or she should live an exemplary life, striving to offer a model of leadership skills and attempting to work with and develop every district coach in their care.

3. They are to prayerfully and tactfully lead all of the district coaches in his or her care to mature, serve and lead to their maximum. This includes setting an example and motivating each district coach to do the same.

4. He or she district coaches' coordinator will keep the small group pastor fully apprised of developments within the districts under their care in a timely manner.

Appendix F:
CareRings Host/Hostess Position Description

- *Take advantage of any hospitality training which is offered in the church.*

- *Arrange for comfortable home (restaurant or business place) for the meetings.*

- *Set up coffee, etc., before the meeting time.*

- *Arrange chairs in cooperation with the Shepherd-Leader(s).*

- *Have a few extra Bibles and pencils for those who forget theirs.*

- *Show people where to put coats, location of restrooms, etc.*

- *Set the atmosphere of love and acceptance for everyone— regular attenders and guest.*

- *Wait until everyone has left before cleaning up and rearranging furniture.*

Appendix G:
CareRings Shepherd-Leader Position Description

- Make a home visit or phone call to all prospects, members (when in need), and referrals from the church office.

- Work with the Host/Hostess to make people comfortable and relaxed.

- Talk and pray with the Apprentice-Shepherd and Host/Hostess before each meeting.

- Report to the District Coach regularly on the development of the Apprentice-Shepherd, remembering that he/she is a potential Shepherd-Leader.

- Initiate the conversational prayer. Lead the Bible application and discussion.

- Be responsible for reporting on the CareRing meeting.

- Pray at the altar immediately when a CareRing member goes forward for prayer in a church service.

Appendix H:
CareRings Apprentice-Shepherd Position Description

- Make a home visit or phone call to all prospects, referrals and potential members.

- Open the meeting.

    ☐ Introduce guests

    ☐ Lead an "ice-breaker" activity for example:
    - "Today was a good day because ..."
    - "My favorite color is ..."
    - "My favorite time of day is ..."
    - "One good thing that's happened since the last meeting is ..."
    - "My favorite junk food is ..."

- Make the announcements the group needs to know about.

- Plan the refreshment schedule.

- Arrange for baby-sitting.

- Lead the lesson and discussion occasionally on request of the Shepherd-Leader.

- Complete and return the CareRing Meeting Report sheet to the District Coach.

NOTES

Chapter One: The Indispensable Ministry

1. William D. Hendricks, *Exit Interviews* (Chicago: Moody Press, 1993), p. 252.
2. Leith Anderson, *A Church for the 21st Century* (Minneapolis: Bethany, 1992), p. 56.
3. Frank R. Tillapaugh, *Unleashing the Church: Getting People out of the Fortress and into Ministry* (Ventura, CA: Regal, 1985); Ray C. Stedman, *Body Life*, rev. ed. (Uhrichsville, OH: Barbour, 1995).
4. Richard C. Halverson, *The Timelessness of Jesus Christ: His Relevance in Today's World* (Ventura, CA: Regal, 1982).
5. The three L's are similar to Peter Wagner's "celebration," "congregation," and "cell." I have turned to the more practical terms for two reasons: (1) The idea of a "cell" is confusing to some people. It conjures up visions of jail or some other small cubicle. (2) The term "congregation" may misdirect some into thinking of the more common usage meaning the whole church in general—not primarily the time and setting in which they meet for praise and worship.

Chapter Two: The Amazing Power of Groups

1. Carl George, *Prepare Your Church for the Future* (Grand Rapids, MI: Revell, 1992), p. 87.
2. Fred H. Smith, "Measuring Quality Church Growth" (Ph.D. dissertation, Fuller Theological Seminary, 1985). David A. Slamp, "The Spirituality Factor: A Vital Dimension of Church Growth" (D.Min. dissertation, Fuller Theological Seminary, 1989). My dissertation contained data drawn from a national study of 1800 people. They were an 11 percent cream sampling representing churches with a total of 25,000 attendees. The Church Growth Institute of Forest, Virginia has published an instrument called "Spiritual Growth Survey" based on this survey.
3. Rosalind Rinker, *Teaching Conversational Prayer* (Waco, TX: Word, 1970).

Chapter Three: CareRings in Context

1. Barry A. Woodbridge, *A Guidebook for Spiritual Friends* (Nashville: Upper Room, 1985).

Chapter Five: Mission Accomplished

1. A full year of the "Guidelines" is available from Serendipity House. It includes master sheets for both participants and leaders that can be copied.

Chapter Six: A Perfect Match

1. Statistics compiled by Central Community Church, Wichita, KS. As a community church, this fellowship has individuals attending irregularly and only for worship services, making follow-up extra difficult.
2. Dr. Toler uses these statistics in his seminar "The Model Church," sponsored by InJoy Ministries, Atlanta, GA.
3. I recently developed a seminar for pastors called "Unleashing the Middle-Sized Church," which trains leaders to expand the leadership base of their congregations. If you think this seminar might be of use to your church, call me at (316) 729-2597.

Chapter Eight: First Steps

1. Dan Southerland, *Transitioning: Leading Your Church through Change* (Grand Rapids, MI: Zondervan, 2000). This book is available through Serendipity House.
2. An excellent resource for district coaches is *Coaches' Handbook*, edited by Bill Donohue of Willow Creek.

Chapter Nine: Decisions, Decisions

1. A one-hour training seminar on leading a turbo-group is available. It includes specific creative ways to inspire and teach potential leaders. It also includes a four-week format and easy instructions to follow that provide all you need to lead a turbo-group. Contact the author at dkslamp@cox.net.

Chapter Ten: Your Other Job

1. Mike Shepherd, *Leadership Development Seminar,* Littleton, CO: January 2000.

Chapter Eleven: A Wagon Built on the Go

1. For a refresher on these regularly scheduled leadership meetings, see chapter seven.
2. Willow Creek Community Church, 67 East Algonquin Road, South Barrington, IL 60010, (847) 765-5000 *www.willowcreek.org.*
3. Saddleback Church, 1 Saddleback Parkway, Lake Forest, CA 92630, (949) 609-8000; *www.saddleback.org.*
4. Southeast Christian Church, 920 Blankenbaker Parkway, Louisville, KY 40243, (502) 253-8000; *secc.org.*
5. Skyline Church, 11330 Campo Rd., La Mesa, CA 91941, (619) 660-5000 www.skylinechurch.org; New Hope Community Church, 11731 SE Stevens Road, Portland, OR 97266, (503) 659-5683; *www.newhopecommunitychurch.org*; Flamingo Road Church, 12401 Stirling Road, Fort Lauderdale, FL 33330, (954) 434-1500; *www.flamingoroad.org;* Central Community Church, 6100 Maple Street, Wichita, KS 67209, (316) 943-1800 *www.centralcommunity.org.*
6. For information on how to attend a CareRings seminar at Central Community Church, call the church at (316) 943-1800.

Chapter Twelve: The Never-Ending Adventure

1. Your church may also want to have an initial training experience for District Shepherds. Experience has proven to me that, no matter how effectively a person may have served in the role of a Shepherd, he or she may not automatically serve as effectively in the role of a District Shepherd. You can follow the same steps in the "path to leadership" for the District Shepherd as for the Shepherd, with the possible exception of skipping the pastoral approval step. I have also written a 4–5 hour training seminar for District coaches which is available by contacting the author, dk_slamp@yahoo.com.

BIBLIOGRAPHY

Aldrich, Joe. *Lifestyle Evangelism: Learning to Open Your Life to Those Around You.* Sisters, OR: Questar, 1993.

Arnold, Jeffrey. *The Big Book on Small Groups.* Downers Grove, IL: InterVarsity Press, 1992.

Bilezikian, Gilbert. *Community 101: Reclaiming the Church as Community of Oneness.* Grand Rapids, MI: Zondervan, 1997.

Bradley, John, and Jay Carty. *Unlocking Your Sixth Suitcase: How to Love What You Do and Do What You Love.* Colorado Springs, CO: NavPress, 1991.

Cho, Paul Yonggi, and Harold Hostetler. *Successful Home Cell Groups.* Plainfield, NJ: Logos, 1981.

Coleman, Lyman. *Serendipity Youth Ministry Encyclopedia.* Littleton, CO: Serendipity, n.d.

Coleman, Robert E. *The Master Plan of Evangelism.* 30th anniv. ed. Grand Rapids, MI: Revell, 1993.

Comiskey, Joel. *Leadership Explosion.* Houston, TX: Touch, 2000.

Crabb, Larry. *Connecting: Healing Ourselves and Our Relationships.* Nashville, TN: Word, 1997.

_____. *The Safest Place on Earth: Where People Connect and Are Forever Changed.* Nashville, TN: Word, 1999.

Donahue, Bill. *The Willow Creek Guide to Leading Life-Changing Small Groups.* Grand Rapids, MI: Zondervan, 1996.

_____. *Coaches Handbook.* South Barrington, IL: Willow Creek Community Church, 1995.

Frazee, Randy. *The Connecting Church: Beyond Small Groups to Authentic Community.* Grand Rapids, MI: Zondervan, 2001.

George, Carl. *Prepare Your Church for the Future.* Grand Rapids, MI: Revell, 1992.

Gorman, Julie A. *Community That Is Christian: A Handbook on Small Groups.* Wheaton, IL: Victor, 1993.

_____. *A Training Manual for Small Group Leaders.* Wheaton, IL: Victor, 1991.

Hamlin, Judy. *The Small Group Leader's Training Course: Trainer's Manual.* Colorado Springs, CO: NavPress, 1990.

Henkelmann, Ervin F., and Stephen J. Carter. *How to Develop a Team Ministry and Make It Work.* St. Louis, MO: Concordia, 1985.

Hestenes, Roberta. *Turning Committees into Communities.* Colorado Springs, CO: NavPress, 1984.

Hunter, George C. III. *How to Reach Secular People.* Nashville, TN: Abingdon, 1992.
Hybels, Lynne, and Bill Hybels. *Rediscovering Church.* Grand Rapids, MI: Zondervan, 1995.
Icenogle, Gareth. *Biblical Foundations for Small Group Ministry: An Integrative Approach.* Downers Grove, IL: InterVarsity Press, 1994.
Johnson, David W., and Frank P. Johnson. *Joining Together: Group Theory and Group Skills.* Needham Heights, MA: Allyn & Bacon, 1994.
Kelley, Robert. *The Power of Followership: How to Create Leaders People Will Want to Follow, and Followers Who Lead Themselves.* New York: Doubleday, 1992.
Larson, Carl E., and Frank M. J. LaFasto. *Teamwork: What Must Go Right, What Can Go Wrong.* Newbury Park, CA: Sage, 1989.
Long, Jimmy, et al. *Small Group Leaders' Handbook.* Downers Grove, IL: InterVarsity Press, 1995.
McBride, Neal F. *How to Have Great Small Group Meetings: Dozens of Ideas You Can Use Right Now.* Colorado Springs, CO.: NavPress, 1997.
_____. *How to Lead Small Groups.* Colorado Springs, CO: NavPress, 1984.
McGavran, Donald A. *Understanding Church Growth.* 3d ed. Grand Rapids, MI: Eerdmans, 1990.
Miller, C. John. *Outgrowing the Ingrown Church.* Grand Rapids, MI: Zondervan, 1986.
Peck, Scott M. *The Different Drum: Community Making and Peace.* New York: Simon & Schuster, 1987.
Schaller, Lyle E. *Creative Leadership Series.* Nashville, TN: Abingdon, 1982.
Slaughter, Michael. *Real Followers.* Nashville, TN: Abingdon, 1999.
Southerland, Dan. *Transitioning: Leading Your Church through Change.* Grand Rapids, MI: Zondervan, 1999.
Wagner, C. Peter. *Leading Your Church to Growth.* Ventura, CA: Regal, 1984.
Watson, David Lowes. *Covenant Discipleship: Christian Formation through Mutual Accountability.* Nashville: Discipleship Resources, 1991.
_____. *The Early Methodist Class Meeting: Its Origins and Significance.* Nashville: Discipleship Resources, 1991.
Wirt, Sherwood Eliot, ed. *Spiritual Witness: Classic Christian Writings of the Twentieth Century.* Wheaton, IL: Crossway, 1991.

Dr. David Slamp has earned the right to be heard. He pastored 25 years, taught in the religion departments of two Christian Universities, authored 3 books, various Bible studies, and served on the staffs as Small Group and Community Pastor in churches of up to 5,100 members!

Dave pioneered the innovative CareRing approach to life-giving community groups in which the groups coordinate and link-up with Bible studies or the Sunday school to maximize life transformation. He has a passion for authentic community building and believes his life call is to, "...equip the saints for the work of ministry." As a result, he has been invited to speak for more than a dozen regional ministry conferences throughout the United States and consults regularly for districts and local churches on two continents.

Dr. Slamp teaches small group dynamics and leadership throughout the US and Africa in many denominations. He has an M.Div. from Nazarene Theological Seminary and earned his doctorate from Fuller Theological Seminary in spiritual formation. He has twice been elected to Who's Who and wrote, the Bearing Spiritual Fruit small group Bible Study, (Ephesians Four Ministries, 2011), The Spiritual Growth Survey, with which pastors and church leaders evaluate the spiritual climate and maturity of congregations. (Published, CGI Press, 1998), and the Spiritual Fruit Assessment. He has been national seminar trainer for Serendipity House for three years.

He lives in Vancouver, WA with his wife, Kathy. They have two grown children, Scott and his wife, Linda and their two children, and Dana who lives in New York City.

To contact Dave Slamp for consultation or speaking invitations:

Email: Dr. David A Slamp **dk_slamp@yahoo.com**

Address: 5713 NE 62nd. Circle
           Vancouver, WA 98661

Website: **www.careringministries.com**

www.ingramcontent.com/pod-product-compliance
Ingram Content Group UK Ltd.
Pitfield, Milton Keynes, MK11 3LW, UK
UKHW022228230426
12048UKWH00016BA/1126